A Modern Parable
Part 1

The Fountain of Money

By

P.D. WELLS

'Knowledge is knowing a tomato is a fruit.
Wisdom is knowing not to put it into a fruit salad.' –
Miles Kington

Dedicated to you.

Copyright 2016 P.D. Wells.
Manuscript consultant and editor Dr Peter Merrington. Published by P.D. Wells at Smashwords.
First published 2016.

PLEASE NOTE: This is a work of fiction. Names, characters, places and incidents are either the product of the author's imagination or are used fictitiously, and any resemblance to actual persons, living or dead, business establishments, events or locales is entirely co-incidental.

The Fountain of Money

Contents

Chapter 1. Destiny

Chapter 2. Flight

Chapter 3. The Company Gardens

Chapter 4. Greed

Chapter 5. Dr Swan

Chapter 6. Fish Hoek Beach

Chapter 7. Big Julius

Chapter 8. Ray Abrahams

Chapter 9. Mrs. Rose Blumkin

Chapter 10. Pay It Forward

Author's note

Chapter 1. Destiny

Destiny, floating high above planet Earth, was worried.

When she had provided the apple on the Tree of Knowledge she had hoped to create a physical Shangri-La for souls to enjoy when they visited the planet earth. But in her haste to speed up evolution she had made a mistake. Unnoticed, greed had slipped in, and since that day it had grown to such an extent that it now threatened to overwhelm the planet, and all who lived there. She had to do something - but what?

Forced to reconsider her strategy, she pondered her options. While she acknowledged that extinction events could be useful solutions, experience had taught her that it would be a very long time before the next window of opportunity opened. And, she reminded herself, the final whistle had not yet blown. She still had one last card to play – she could provide a Tree of Wisdom.

However, in order to deliver this message she would need an emissary. This would have to be a very special person.

After studying the planet for a long time she finally found a likely candidate.

Chapter 2. Flight

Forced to flee the City of Gold, Ash returned to the only place he understood - home. And getting there involved flying, which he feared.

In order to elude his debtors he arrived at O R Tambo airport early and quickly checked in. Hoping to ease his fear of flying he reserved a window seat. He hoped that this, and a few calming pills, would settle his phobia.

With his boarding pass securely in his pocket he found a quiet corner in a restaurant, ordered a coffee, opened the newspaper and disappeared from view.

While taking an order at the next table the waitress dropped her pen. It bounced across the floor and rolled under Ash's table.
Being a gentleman he bent down to retrieve it but he couldn't reach it. So, he got down on his hands and knees and crawled under the table. When he returned the pen to the waitress she blushed.

The customer whom she was serving had a ring-side seat and appreciated Ash's chivalry. He caught Ash's eye, raised his finger to his brow and smiled. Ash gave a brief nod of acknowledgement and returned to his hiding place. Then he swallowed a few calming pills.

By the time his flight was called the pills had taken effect. He was relaxed and he felt as if he were floating. He joined the queue, boarded the plane and took his seat. Staring out the window, he studied the sky. A dark storm was drawing closer. It unnerved him.

While the passengers were boarding Ash kept an eye open to see who would be seated next to him. Much to his relief, nobody came. But just as the cabin door was about to close one last passenger arrived. The late-comer was a small, clean-shaven man who weaved his way quickly up the aisle and headed straight for the empty seat next to Ash.

Examining his boarding pass, he checked the seat number, looked at Ash, smiled and sat down. Having made himself comfortable he addressed Ash:

"Hey, that was kind of you!"

Ash didn't understand what the stranger meant.

"The waitress with the pen, remember? She was serving me."

Oh, great, thought Ash. *There goes my cover.*

"TK," said the man extending his hand.

Ash felt awkward and acknowledged TK's greeting with a grunt. Then he turned and looked out the window again. A storm was approaching.

The plane taxied to the runway and a firm female voice came over the intercom: "Since we will be flying close to a thunderstorm the captain requests that you kindly remain seated and keep your seatbelts fastened throughout the flight. We will be landing in Cape Town in two hours, where we expect good weather and a pleasant evening."

Ash took this as a warning and his chest started to constrict. He didn't hear the safety instructions that followed. He stared out of the window to calm his mind, but the storm-clouds were closing in.

The plane came to a halt at the end of the runway and the pilot revved the engines. As the plane shuddered and strained at its leash the tightness in Ash's chest grew. The pilot released the brakes, the plane sprang forward and Ash felt his heart rate quicken. He looked out of the window - the grass on the edge of the runway moved past, faster and faster. Little beads of sweat appeared on his forehead.

As the white lines on the runway began to blur his hands tightened their grip on the arm rests. The nose of the plane lifted and his legs went rigid. He strained against the seat belt. The plane rose into the sky. Lightning flashed against the dark storm-clouds and the plane was buffeted by strong winds. Ash found it hard to breath. The plane hit turbulence and groaned and shuddered. Ash began to sweat profusely. The plane hit an air pocket and dropped. Ash's fingers grabbed his tie and ripped it off. Then, just as panic took hold, Ash saw a blinding flash of light and his world went silent.

"Relax, mate, relax," called a gentle voice. "Breathe."

The plane hit the bottom of the air pocket with a crash.

"Steady, mate, steady," soothed the voice. "Don't stress. Breathe."

The voice revived him and slowed his panic.

Slowly the claustrophobia relaxed its grip on his chest and his mind began to clear.

"Try and stretch your toes down, and see if you can touch the earth," said the voice. "You will feel much better."

Ash tried, and it seemed to work. Thought slowly returned to him. He came around and seemed confused - as if he had just awakened from a dream and was surprised to find himself sitting on a plane. He felt as if he had been away – as if he had gone to a very quiet place with a bright white light. He was stunned.

Slowly Ash became aware of the gentle hum of the engines and the hushed conversations around him. The man called TK, sitting next to him with the soothing voice, looked worried. The air hostess, who had been watching Ash, hurried over with two bottles of water.

"Thank you," she said to TK.

"No problem," said TK, but his eyes told a different story.

Ash took a sip of water and shook his head.

"You don't like flying?"

"No," said Ash shaking his head again. "Not at all; take-off and landings terrify me."

"And flying itself?"

"I can deal with that."

TK breathed a sigh of relief and sat back in his seat.

"I'm grateful for this water," said Ash, mopping his brow. "Please excuse my panic. I try to control my fear but thunderstorms and air pockets freak me out."

"If I thought about it," replied TK, "I'd probably react the same way. But fortunately I don't think about it."

Without excusing himself Ash turned his face to the window and disappeared into his thoughts. The impression of the white light was still vivid and he remained stunned by the power of his out-of-body experience. Was this a message from the Great Beyond?

Like the plane as it passed through the air, he was passing through life. He had made mistakes. His business empire had collapsed. He had been humiliated, he was broke, and his self-image shattered. He was however - still alive.

He who had flown so high was now humbled - cast down to feed on the ground with the pigeons. This humbling was a difficult pie to eat and Ash doubted if he had the strength to endure the shame of it. Ending his life seemed to be a reasonable proposition. He'd reviewed his options. Drowning seemed the easiest way to go. He could make it look like an accident.

Unbeknown to Ash, Destiny was in charge. She presided over events and she was firmly in control. It was she who had brought him to this crossroads. And now that he'd been tenderized Ash was ready to begin the next chapter in his life.

"Disasters are good," said TK. "That's how we learn."

"I guess so," replied Ash.

"I hope you've avoided the fate of so many others."

"What fate is that?" asked Ash warily.

"When their careers end abruptly they find they are broke."

Ash was lost in his thoughts and the words popped out of his mouth before his brain had time to edit them. "That's me," he confessed.

"What do you mean?"

"I'm broke."

"I don't get it," said TK. He looked puzzled. At first Ash didn't respond. He gazed down on the world floating miles below, and then with a sigh, he spoke:

"I've learned that I'm a fool."

TK raised his eyebrows.

"When I got my break I was too young to know what to do with all the money." There was an exhausted sadness in his voice. "I didn't know how to cope and was too cock-sure to ask for advice. I spent my fortune as if the tap would never run dry. But it did."

"You're not dumb," responded TK trying to cheer him up.

"Thank you," said Ash. "That's kind of you. But I was stupid."

"What happened?"

"While the going was good I had many friends, but as soon as the hard times arrived they disappeared," said Ash sadly.

"By the time I woke up I was deeply in debt with nothing to show. I hoped to recover and settle my debts, build a nest egg, get married, but then along came the GFC and whoosh – all gone."

"The GFC?

"The Global Financial Crisis."

"Of course," said TK nodding in sympathy. "And what's left for you now?"

Ash grunted: "A pile of debts and some memories."

"Will you ever return to the City of Gold?"

"I doubt it," said Ash curtly.

"So what now?" asked TK, slowly baiting the hook.

Ash felt that TK was asking too many personal questions. He wanted to keep his misfortune to himself. However, despite his best efforts to shut his mouth, the honest answers kept tumbling out.

"I'll have to start again. But I don't know where."

"Don't be too hard on yourself," said TK. "There's good news."

"What could that be?"

"You've learned how to recognize a gift horse."

"Huh?" grunted Ash as he stared at TK with astonishment. "All I've done is lose them."

"What I mean is that you seem to have learned from your mistakes."

"That is true," said Ash conceding the point. "But it's been an expensive lesson."

"Failure is part of the journey. It contributes to success."

"I tried to fly too high," admitted Ash, opening up to the stranger despite himself. "My wings melted."

"We all need humbling."

Ash was getting irritated. He didn't need to have the obvious rubbed in even deeper.

"All is definitely not lost," said TK. He spoke more brightly.

"What do you mean?" responded Ash. His voice was sharp. Couldn't the man see that he, Ash, was stuffed? Finished, kaput, game over. He only had two choices left to him: humble pie or a big swim. Neither of which appealed to him.

"You've only lost your cash," said TK quietly. "And we can only become truly wealthy once we've learned the value of what we *do* have."

Ash shrugged his shoulders. More platitudes. "I guess that's true," he muttered.

"So - now that you've arrived at this crossroads – isn't it a good time to take stock?"

"What do you mean?"

"Isn't this a good time to ask what you truly want out of life?"

Ash looked at TK with suspicion. He didn't like trick questions. They made him nervous. Neither did he like it when strangers got this familiar. But TK made an excellent point - he had never defined what he really wanted out of life. Maybe now was a good time.

"You have experience," continued TK, "but you are broke. In essence, this leaves you free to decide what you really want."

"You didn't need a disaster to realize this - the 'popcorn moment' is always present. But in most cases, such as yours, it usually does take a disaster to help you make up your mind. And that seems to be what you've chosen - a disaster, the difficult path, to help you wake up. So it is – here you are."

TK paused and looked Ash in the eye: "Well? Have you found an answer to my question?"

"What question?"

"What do you want from life?"

Once again exasperation overcame Ash, and he glared at TK. He didn't like where this conversation was going but he was being swept along by the spell of the white light; and there was little he could do about it.

"Do you have a destination in mind?" persisted TK.

"No," admitted Ash.

"Well, without a destination there can't be any journey."

"I suppose you're right," said Ash nodding.

"To know your destination you must first define what you want from life. Then you can develop a plan that will make it real."

Ash looked down at the world drifting below the clouds. Maybe he did have some options. Humiliation, he admitted, was no easy pill to swallow, and TK was hinting at a possible silver lining. Maybe he could hold off on that big swim for a while.

"Want do you want most out of life?" prompted TK, not allowing Ash to settle.

"I want to be wealthy," replied Ash without hesitation.

"But what does wealth mean to you?"

Ash dug in his heels. "You're wealthy when you have a lot of money," he said.

"Only money?" queried TK.

"Without money, you're stuffed." Ash looked at TK as if he came from another planet.

"Describe wealth," challenged TK.

"When you've got a lot of money!"

"Is that all? Just money?" TK casually examined his fingernails. "What does it take for you to be content with your life? Financial freedom is important, but it's not everything."

For a moment Ash looked as if he were about to explode. "I don't buy that. Without money you are well and truly stuffed."

"Real wealth," said TK gently, "includes financial security, but it also includes love, a family, a home, friends, and a healthy environment. Go on - think about it. If you ask what is meant by true wealth - surely you mean a good lifestyle? Being free of stress? Being at peace with yourself? At peace with life?"

"Fair enough," conceded Ash. "I guess so." He was slowly warming to the conversation, but he remained septical. "Right now all those lovely things seem a very long way off."

"Not really," said TK dangling the hook a little closer.

"All I can do right now," insisted Ash, "is think about earning enough money to survive. The other stuff is all just add-on."

Ash couldn't see it any other way.

"That's the whole thing," said TK. "People are taught how to work for money, not how money can work for them."

This comment stopped Ash in his tracks. He studied TK carefully. *Was this guy for real?*

"Look, there's a very simple way in which money can be made to work for you."

"How?" asked Ash, nibbling at the baited hook.

"Simple. Create a fountain of money."

A fountain of money - the image leaped into Ash's brain. It spoke to him. He liked the idea of having his own personal fountain of money. If he could, he would have ordered a whole bunch of them yesterday.

"It's simple," said TK in a matter-of-fact voice. "Even if you are poor you can become wealthy."

"*Yeah right*," said Ash sarcastically.

"Financial security is available to everybody – and it doesn't matter how difficult your circumstances are, everybody can be financially free."

"Tell me another one."

"You don't believe me," said TK smiling confidently. "It's easy. All you need to be is consistent and patient and you will become financially free."

Yeah, yeah, thought Ash. He needed a miracle, not more platitudes.

But TK wouldn't let go. "Financial security is available to all."

Ridiculous! thought Ash and looked out of the window again.

"If you follow the rules, you can create your own personal Shangri-La."

Though Ash did not realize it then, years later, when he looked back over his life, he came to realize that this was the moment when it changed forever.

"There is a practical, easy-to-implement way to create great wealth," continued TK.

"What's that?" said Ash adjusting his seat to the upright position.

"The secret of the Money Fountain."

Ash started paying closer attention.

"There are three aspects to a Money Fountain," said TK, his fingers forming a triangle. "Each aspect has its own operating system. Once you get all three operating systems in place and working together, your Money Fountain will start producing."

Ash saw an image of a fountain spewing out dollar bills.

"And the longer you stick to the rules, the faster the fountain will flow."

Ash saw a mighty deluge of dollars streaming towards him like a river bursting its banks.

"Eventually, you will struggle to give the money away."

Ash saw himself giving away bundles and bundles of cash to thousands of happy people. But how was this possible?

"All you have to do is keep to the rules," said TK.

That sounded very simple, and Ash was keen to know more.

"Getting everything into line isn't easy," cautioned TK. "But when you do your Money Fountain will start flowing. It works."

"Follow the rules and you will create a never-ending stream of wealth. You will never be poor again."

"If that's the case," challenged Ash, "Why doesn't everybody know about this?"

"The reason you don't know about how a Money Fountain works," said TK firmly, "is because others are putting your money to work in their Money Fountain - and they don't want you to know about this."

"Excuse me?" said Ash leaning closer. *Was he being cheated?*

"Financial institutions invest your money in their own Money Fountains, and then they give you returns of a small interest rate to keep you quiet."

Ash looked stunned. It was a new way of looking at things. "Is that why they're rich, and we aren't?"

"Exactly," said TK confidently. "But when you create your own Money Fountain your money will work for you, and not for somebody else. It's a simple matter of taking control of your finances - and your life."

"You mean - empowering myself?"

"Exactly," said TK.

Ash felt like he had just been slapped. It sounded so obvious. *Why hadn't he realized this before?*

"Then how can I create a Money Fountain for myself?"

"The system's simple – and it works," said TK moving the baited hook out of range.

"Could you teach me how to create one?" asked Ash, lunging for the bait.

"Depends," said TK, becoming evasive. If Ash wanted to know more he would have to show some commitment. How much fight did he have? Destiny was also keen to test his resolve. And knowing Ash's fear of landing, she prodded the air hostess into action.

"Please stow your cabin baggage and fasten your seatbelts. We'll be landing in Cape Town in ten minutes."

The air hostess's voice brought back Ash's fear of flying, and he promptly forgot all about the Money Fountain.

"Relax, Ash. Breathe. Be gentle," said TK quietly. "Stretch your toes down – all the way - and see if you can touch the earth."

Ash tried. He found that if he imagined it he could stretch his toes all the way down and touch the earth - and when they touched, he found that he could breathe again.

His hands relaxed their grip on the armrests. He took a sip of water and looked out of the window. Soon the city lights became visible.
The plane approached the airport and the lights below resolved themselves into strings of fairy lanterns. These were strung out against the dark silhouette of Table Mountain, which was etched on a sky of gold. Ash was coming home - broken and broke.

And yet the flight had panned out to be more than he'd expected. He'd seen a white light, a glimmer of a silver lining, and a Money Fountain. Was this a genuine gift horse? Was this a new path opening before him?

"It was nice meeting you, Ash."

"Thank you," said Ash, but as TK started to get up Ash interrupted him. "Would you be prepared to teach me about the Money Fountain?"

"Maybe."

"No," insisted Ash. "I'm serious. "I've been humbled. I acknowledge it. I believe I've learned my lesson."

"Maybe you have," said TK. "Here's my card. Call me. The ball's in your court."

Chapter 3. The Company Gardens

A few days later when Ash caught the bus into Cape Town he had an enthusiastic spring in his step.

TK had agreed to teach him how to create a Money Fountain and he was on his way to meet him at one of his favorite places, the restaurant in the Company Gardens in the heart of Cape Town.

He alighted at the City Hall and walked up to the gardens through the old city. He enjoyed the narrow streets, exotic aromas and small shops. He walked up Parliament Street and emerged in Church Square, the old slave market. Naively he walked beneath a gnarled old tree - under which the slaves had squatted while waiting to be sold. Then he turned right into Spin Street and walked past the Slave Lodge, a building with an awfully dark history.
Though he had no idea about any of these horrid details, they were his history. And he had no idea that he himself might still be enslaved.

This realization lay in the future.

On the corner of Adderley Street he turned left and glanced up Government Avenue - a pedestrian mall shaded by oak trees and fringed with beds of agapanthus. To his right towered the dark stone bulk of St George's Cathedral. On his left were the Houses of Parliament. These had been painted a dark maroon with white trim, and now looked like a brightly decorated gingerbread house.

As Ash walked up the shaded avenue squirrels and pigeons begged alms off him, but Ash shook his head. Pathetically, he did not even have enough money to buy a paper bag of peanuts from the peanut vendor.

The sheer three-thousand-foot rock face of Table Mountain reared up into the sky. At the east and west ends of the mountain, two peaks - Lion's Head and Devil's Peak – seemed to cradle the Company Gardens down below, in an eternal embrace.

When he entered the Company Gardens time slowed down and nature asserted itself above the hubbub of the city.
The garden was tranquil and filled with the sound of birds and tinkling fountains. The lawns were neatly trimmed and edged with bright flower beds, set against a backdrop of shaded groves of large old trees.

The coral trees were in full bloom, as was the magnolia.
Ash walked slowly through the dripping vines of the Japanese pagoda and emerged at the entrance to the outdoor eatery.

TK was already seated at a table and being served a cup of coffee. When he saw Ash, he smiled and waved.

"Would you like a coffee?" he asked, as Ash seated himself.

"Yes please. That would be great."

TK placed the order and Ash looked around. The outdoor space was dominated by a large gum tree. The green plastic tables and chairs were cheap and faded and looked like they came from a suburban garden.

A flock of pigeons patrolled the paving stones below the table, looking for morsels that fell from the plates of the affluent. Ash empathized - these guys were now his mates. He was on their team.

"So," began TK, "where are we?"

"I find myself at a crossroads," said Ash. "And I can only choose which road to take when I know my destination."

"And what destination would that be?"

"I would like to create a Money Fountain for myself! And I'm hoping that you'll teach me."

"Excellent," said TK. "Every journey begins with the first step – and this is exactly where you are."

Ash's cappuccino arrived. He noticed that the foam was full of bubbles. It looked thin and almost transparent. He opened a sachet of sugar and poured it onto the foam. The sugar sank straight through and disappeared.

"That happens when the milk's too hot," said TK. He pointed at the bubbles in the foam. "If you want to make perfect foam, the milk mustn't get hotter than 145° Fahrenheit. And when you make foam for a cappuccino you're only meant to skim the top of the milk with the steam. That's the screaming noise you hear. But the person who made this foam didn't know that and inserted the nozzle into the milk and boiled it. That's why there are bubbles in the foam."

Ash frowned and examined the bubbles in the foam.

"Good foam," continued TK, "should have very fine silky bubbles. It should appear solid and it should be able to support the weight of a sachet of sugar."

"To be honest," he added, "the coffee here isn't good. It's more like an excuse for coffee. But that's completely unimportant. I come here for the fresh air, the birds, the mountain, the fountains and … today, I come here for you."

Ash was humbled. He thanked TK. He steered the conversation back to his quest.

"About the Money Fountain," he said. "I'm keen to know more."

"Ah yes, the Money Fountain," murmured TK. "How to create a stream of money that flows endlessly towards you in such a manner that the flow grows bigger and faster with each passing day?"

"That's the one," said Ash. He nodded keenly.

"I'll be honest with you," replied TK. "Creating a Money Fountain isn't easy. It'll take time and dedication. Are you prepared for such a commitment?"

"I'll do my best," said Ash.

"You'll have to do better than that," said TK. "If you want a Money Fountain you have to stick to the rules, or it won't work."

Ash swallowed and focused. He now realized that TK wasn't mucking around.

"Wealth," announced TK, "comes from hard work, diligence, consistent saving and considered investments. Creating great wealth is a measured approach, and after twenty-five years you'll be financially independent."

"Twenty-five years?"

"Yes," said TK. "Are you still interested?"

"Well, yes....."

"If you like, I will mentor you."

"How much will it cost?"

"Nothing," said TK. "But whatever I teach you, you are obliged to pay-it-forward."

"What's that?"

"Whatever you receive for free, you will in turn give for free. Is that fair?"

"It sounds fair," said Ash.

"Then your word is taken as final?"

"Accepted," said Ash. The two men shook hands.

"Welcome aboard," said TK happily. "Now I can introduce you to the Fellowship."

"The Fellowship?" asked Ash.

"Yes," said TK. "There are quite a few of us. We all belong to a movement that seeks to create wealth that is good for people and for the planet. We call it Conscious Wealth."

"Wealth that's good for the planet? Is that possible?"

"Indeed it is," said TK confidently. "Remember - without a destination, there can't be a journey."

"Yes," said Ash nodding. "That is correct."

"So the first thing to do is to establish a destination, and then plan how to get there."

"So, what is that destination?" asked Ash.

"Our ultimate destination is to create wealth that is good for the planet - and good for people too. And we do this by creating Money Fountains."
"And when millions of Money Fountains flow together to the same destination," continued TK, "they create wonders. This is what we call Conscious Wealth. And the beauty of this system is that it's not based on usury."

"Usury? What's that?"

"Usury is when you lend money to people for interest. It's an ancient practice which was forbidden by some religions and societies. It's greed. It's like renting out money to another person who has to pay back the capital along with rental costs. You know how it works, of course. When you take out an overdraft at the bank or borrow on a credit card, you end up paying back a lot more than the capital sum. You pay the lender interest on a predetermined scale. You bleed. The other party makes a nice profit off your bleeding."

"So if you don't charge interest then how does the Money Fountain create money?" asked Ash.

"From dividends," said TK. "And that is the beauty of a Money Fountain and Conscious Wealth."

"I think I understand," said Ash taking a sip of his coffee.

"So the first thing to do is to teach you how a Money Fountain works – how to make money work for you, and not you for it."

"I like the sound of that," said Ash with enthusiasm.

"I thought you would," said TK smiling. "Everybody does. But let's begin at the beginning."

"As your mentor, my job is to guide you. I will introduce you to your tutors, and answer your questions. Your tutors will be Dr. Swan, Big Julius, and Mrs. Blumkin. Each is a specialist in a field of wealth creation. If you need more information I'll refer you to other tutors."

"Thank you," said Ash gratefully.

"Once you've been taught, and your Money Fountain begins to work, you will become a member of the team - the Fellowship, bound by the pay-it-forward principle. What we receive for free we are honor-bound to share."

Ash nodded solemnly. He understood. He liked the idea. It sounded fair.

"The Fellowship is committed to bringing financial liberation to the world by creating wealth that is beneficial to the environment."

"But isn't wealth based on exploitation?"

"It doesn't have to be," said TK. "Look at that fountain in the middle of the pond. Is it doing harm? Of course not. Does a natural spring do harm? Of course not. Like a natural spring, the Money Fountain produces wealth that's good for the planet."

Ash was intrigued – and wanted to know more.

"Shall we eat?" invited TK.

Ash was starving but he disguised his hunger with a casual nod. TK scanned the menu. Then, as if speaking to himself, he said, "The food's not that great here. Best to stick to something that everybody knows - something local. Like a curry – a traditional Cape Malay dish – that's the way to go. Is that okay?"

"Great," said Ash. "I'll go with that."

TK waved to the waitress, who was chatting on her mobile. She ended the call and came over to the table.

"Curried lamb bobotie for two please," said TK. "With the usual sambals and two glasses of apple juice."

Turning to Ash he asked: "Is that okay with you? Healthy food - not costly either."

'Wonderful," said Ash. TK confirmed their order and the waitress departed.

"You need to understand," said TK refocusing the conversation, "that wealth isn't just about money. It is also about love and friends and your quality of life. This is all part of a Money Fountain. Enjoy your life. Fall in love. Learn to laugh. Look after your health and your body - because without it you've got nothing." He paused. Then he grinned. "There's a story that goes with this. Do you like stories?"

"Yes," said Ash. "They help me to remember important details."

"Good." TK sat back and folded his arms and legs and began. "One day a genie appears before a young man and says to him, 'Young man, you can have any car you want. Name your choice.'

"The young man is naturally taken by surprise by the genie's sudden appearance and the offer – so he takes some time to reflect on it. Being cautious by nature, he is immediately suspicious. 'Thank you,' he says to the genie, 'this is a very generous offer - but it seems too generous. There must be a catch.'

"The genie is taken aback. He's been caught out so quickly and is obliged to admit that there is indeed a catch.

"'You can only ever have this one car,' he explains, 'and it has to last your whole life.'

"'What do you mean?' asks the young man.

"'Just that,' says the genie. 'You get to choose any car you like, but it has to last a lifetime.'

"The young man thinks about the proposition. He plans to live for a long time, so he realizes that he would have to look after the car very carefully. He would have to garage it, service it regularly, wash it, and if it was in an accident, repair it. As it aged, a flashy sports car would become more and more expensive to maintain. That wouldn't work."

Ash wondered where the story was going. He asked TK if this was a trick question.

"Yes. In a way it is," said TK. He spread his hands in a deprecatory gesture. "The gift the genie is referring to is your body. You only get one, and it has to last a lifetime."

"This is one of the key principles to creating a Money Fountain. Look after your health and emotional well-being. The reason this is important is because we want you to be around to enjoy the fruits of your Money Fountain."

That sounded good and it made Ash smile.

"Money is just a part of wealth," continued TK. "Family, friends, living a life of significance, inner wealth, spirituality, and caring about the environment – these are all important aspects of true wealth. You need to pay them all equal attention. Grow plants and marvel at evolution - because there you'll see God's greatest creation."

The waitress arrived with lunch and placed before them two steaming plates of yellow saffron rice with raisins topped with a rich brown lamb curry. Then she set down between the plates a bowl of sambals. Finally she set down two tall frosted glasses of fresh apple juice, with a sprig of mint. The feast was set.

TK ran his eye over the sambals – the side dishes –small servings of mango and peach chutney, chopped tomato, onion and coriander pickle and a dish with sliced banana sprinkled with lemon juice and coconut shavings – along with a basket of crisp breads.

"Perfect," he said, drawing his chair closer to the table. First he turned his mutton curry lightly with his fork, and smiled. Then he reached for the chutney and spooned it on. Next he added a dash of chopped tomato-and-onion pickle. Then he added some sliced banana in lemon juice on top. A rich curry aroma now rose from this bright meal. Then TK bowed his head and said a silent grace.

Ash got the point. He realized that this was a lesson - a tasty, healthy, attractive lesson about living in the richness of the present moment. While they ate, TK continued to speak.

"There are three aspects to a Money Fountain," said TK while he tucked in. "Pay-Yourself–First or PYF, the Magic Penny, and the Perfect Investment." He glanced up at Ash.

"Doctor Swan, Big Julius and Mrs Blumkin will be your tutors and guide you through each facet."

Ash raised his eyes.

"Yes. These three are the sides of a triangle. When they start working together they create a Money Fountain - your own never-ending stream of wealth. It's pretty much fail-safe." The confidence impressed Ash. "Stick to the rules and you will be financially secure."

"I find that hard to believe," said Ash. He wanted to tuck in – the flavors exploding in his mouth – but he also wanted more reassurance.

"It's a grand statement," said TK. "But it's true."

"That's incredible," said Ash skeptically. "But - what could cause a Money Fountain to stop flowing?"

"Well," replied TK carefully, "the only thing I can think of that could prevent you from achieving your goal is if a meteorite collides with the earth and wipes us all out."

"Oh," said Ash. "In that case it sounds pretty much fail-safe."

TK gave him a knowing smile. "Wealth is attracted to those who save. This is the most important point. Fail here and you may as well put on handcuffs and throw away the key."

"What do you mean?"

"If you can't save then you won't be able to Pay Yourself First. And if that's the case then you will remain enslaved."

"Enslaved?" Ash frowned. "What do you mean?"

"Unless you start saving you will always be poor."

TK returned with relish to his curry. Then he again addressed Ash:

"Here's another story for you. It's about a farm laborer called Jonas."

Ash, who was enjoying his meal, was happy to listen and eat at the same time.

"Jonas wasn't paid well, but he was grateful for the opportunity to work and he enjoyed the fresh air and the company.

"One day while he and his fellow laborers were walking to work, Jonas pointed to the neighbor's fields and commented that the workers on that farm weren't ploughing the fields deeply enough. The point he was trying to make was that the seedlings would find it hard to grow in the shallow trenches, but his workmates didn't see it that way.

"They laughed at him and said that those laborers were wise because who wants to work hard digging deep trenches in return for little pay?

"A discussion began. Jonas tried to justify his position by pointing out that because those laborers were cutting corners they would reap a poor harvest, and this would put their jobs at risk.

"The others jeered at him and Jonas got marked out by his fellow workers as a potential traitor to their cause.

"But that didn't stop Jonas," said TK. "He got great satisfaction from watching crops grow into tall healthy plants. He tried to tell his workmates that hard work and diligence brought good things in life. But they still laughed and jeered at Jonas. They said that only a fool would work hard for such little pay. Jonas ignored them and persisted with his quest.

"The farmer heard the men arguing, but kept quiet. When the crop was harvested the farmer noticed that it fetched a higher price than his neighbor's. Still the farmer said nothing.

"But Jonas was not deterred by the farmer's silence. He had a plan and he continued to work hard.

"In his spare time he learned all there was to learn about the crops that they were planting and the best way to protect the crops from disease and insects. Then he applied his knowledge. The farmer noticed this as well.

"When the next harvest was reaped it again fetched a higher price. This time the farmer gave Jonas a raise and more responsibility. In this way he rose above being an ordinary laborer, but he still enjoyed working and learning.

"The farmer was impressed, and gave Jonas a percentage of the harvest. See what I mean, Ash? Do you get the point? This is how hard work and study attract wealth."

Ash took another sip of his apple juice. It was cool and sweet.

"So," TK prodded him, "what's the moral of the story?"

Ash was still uncertain.

"All good things come from hard work."

Ash pondered the statement, and then reluctantly nodded.

"When you work hard and study to improve your knowledge," continued TK, "you make yourself attractive to employers, and in this way hard work attracts the good things."

TK, who had managed to talk the whole way through his mutton curry, now mopped up the remainder with a crisp piece of bread.
When he finished he neatly set down his knife and fork, pushed his plate to the side and beckoned to the waitress.

"Thank you ma'm," he smiled. "That was delicious. Is your espresso any good?"

"Yes sir. Top class."

"Espresso, Ash?"

"Thank you."

"Two espressos, please, ma'am."

"Coming up."

An explosive boom reverberated across the city, causing the pigeons to fly up in alarm and the fountains to fall silent.

"Ah - the noonday gun," said TK, without missing a beat.

The echo died away, the pigeons returned to their ground patrol and Ash could hear the fountain tinkling once again. Peace returned to the garden.

"Now - whatever you do, please keep away from thoughts of get-rich-quick," said TK. His voice was stern. "Do not buy a lottery ticket."

"Why?" asked Ash.

"Because dreams of big easy wins are most of the time pure fantasy. They don't bring any returns. Wealth creation is a simple, structured plan that requires diligence and commitment."

Ash took a moment to internalize the message and then he finished his meal. He wiped his mouth with his serviette.

"Look, Ash," said TK apologetically, "I've got to fly. But you've got my card. Call me when you're ready and I'll set up the meetings with your tutors. They will explain the operating systems of the Money Fountain to you."

Ash felt downcast. He had hoped to go home with a Money Fountain in his pocket. TK's reference to those tutors suggested time and effort, which he wasn't that keen to commit to.

Destiny noticed this.

"You are too kind," said Ash, though his words were hollow.

"Do you have a car?" asked TK.

"Yes." Ash fibbed again. He had lost everything in the implosion, including his flashy car.

"Good. Big Julius lives a little way away and you will need to drive."

Ash didn't yet believe in the forgiving hand of fate. To him fate seemed to be the enemy. It had caused untold mischief in his life. His life had been a struggle to overcome fate.

But Destiny was present and she was not that impressed with Ash. Quite correctly, she had noticed that Ash was still looking for easy solutions. It seemed to her that he didn't yet fully appreciate the sting of desperation. It seemed to her that another lesson was required.

As Ash made his way to the bus stop a pretty girl stumbled into him on the pavement. He put out his arms to steady her. He noticed her – he couldn't help doing so - but he didn't notice her quick fingers. When he reached into his pocket at the bus stop he found that his wallet was gone - and along with it, TK's card.

Once again, Ash was welcomed back to pain and hardship. His mettle would be tested.

Chapter 4. Greed

Ash drove to Kalk Bay and parked his car, a purple Datsun hatchback, under the Norfolk pines and looked down on the little harbor.

A cold mist had settled over the city and hung over the sea and the harbor. Brightly painted wooden fishing boats were moored against the protecting harbor wall. At the far end of the wall was a quaint lighthouse - Ash's intended destination.

The weather didn't trouble Ash. He liked cold wet days because they kept most folks indoors, and left the best places to him, giving him time and space to be alone with his thoughts. And Ash needed to think.

He'd lost his wallet and, with it, TK. Since that day in the Company Gardens life had led him down a rocky road. He needed to reflect on this. Perhaps today was a good day for that last desperate swim.

Stomping through the puddles he crossed the main road and climbed the stairs to the boardwalk. At the top he stopped and observed the arched railway bridge and the harbor waters lapping the beach.

Some vagrants were packing up their night camp and preparing for a day's carousing.
Funny, Ash thought to himself, how most people struggle to accumulate wealth, yet these people didn't seem to give a hoot about it and were still content. Money wasn't their god.

A train whistle blew. It broke his thought and he looked up in time to see the train slip out of the station. It passed noisily in front him. Ash watched as it as it curved out of sight. Then he crossed the tracks at the level crossing and walked down the short road into the harbor.

The mist hung low and wreathed itself around the tops of the masts of the fishing boats. A boat captain stood smoking at the door of his wheelhouse, directing his crew. Lobster pots were piled high on the sterns of most of the boats. On others nets had been hung out to rinse in the drizzle. The sea gurgled under the pier. A seal surfaced and lay on its back, staring at Ash. Then with a single flip of its tail it glided under the water and disappeared.

Ash passed quietly behind the fishmongers at their stalls and climbed the stairs to the harbor wall. The far side of the wall had been raised to form a stone bench. He climbed up onto the bench and peered over the top of the wall. The dark green sea looked cold, and made him shiver – and as the water rose and fell, it carried on its dark surface a mass of floating kelp.
Ash took a deep breath and fortified himself – it did not look like a good day for a big last swim. And yet....

Ash pulled the hood of his jacket over his head and strolled quietly towards the lighthouse at the end of the pier. A fisherman, huddled under the hood of his parka, sat on the bench dangling his line over the edge. He had a tackle box beside him, a bait bucket, and, optimistically, a bucket for his catch. As Ash hoped, the fisherman didn't see him pass.

Ash got to the end of the pier. He sat down and allowed his feet to dangle over the edge. Watching the waves as they rose and fell just under his feet, he thought it would be a little jump and that would be the end of his troubles. He doubted if the fisherman would even hear his splash.

Once, he'd been rich and famous, but now he was haunted by his losses. He had thrown away his many gift horses. He'd even managed to lose TK.

Four years had passed since that day in the Company Gardens and life had led him down a hard-lonely road. Now he was confused and no longer knew which way to turn.

Ash had eaten his full portion of humble pie and now he was tired of the adversity. He felt like giving up.

He'd tried to put his life back together.
He had secured a job managing a hardware store. He didn't know much about hardware, but he was popular and customers came to the store because of him. The turnover had climbed and shrinkage had fallen, and his boss was pleased with him. Ash was also studying management. His job gave him stability and he was saving up to buy a home. And this was when the hard times had returned into his life.

He had saved some money, but he was impatient because the money that he had deposited in the bank grew too slowly. In order to buy a house he needed to grow his money faster. So one day when his new friend - Selwyn - offered him a chance to break the chains that bound him, he grabbed it.

Selwyn had put together a syndicate that was going to Thailand to buy emeralds, and he invited Ash to buy into the syndicate. At first Ash resisted, but Selwyn begged to be heard out and, since Ash was a gentleman, he relented. For a five-thousand-rand buy-in, Selwyn offered a guaranteed 300 per cent return. Ash had asked for references and had contacted them. They all spoke with confidence.

Ash did not tell anyone when he withdrew his savings. Neither did he mention Selwyn's bring-home-the-bacon-quickly plan. In due course his stones arrived and he set off to consult an expert to have them valued.

While he waited to be seen by the jeweler Ash gazed at the glittering glass-fronted cabinets of gold, diamonds, tanzanite and rubies. He fell in love with a rose-gold pendant and matching earrings with inset rubies. He wished there was a girl in his life, to give them to.

The jeweler called him and Ash handed over his packet of stones. The jeweler affixed a magnifier to his eye and placed the stones under a bright light. Then he examined each stone carefully. After examining all the stones he took the magnifier from his eye and looked at Ash. The sadness in his eyes spoke louder than any words and Ash felt himself falling slowly backwards into a dark cavern long before he heard the words - "fake, glass, sorry".

Somehow Ash found the strength to pick himself up and carry on. He kept his job at the hardware store but he did not tell his boss why Selwyn never came back.

Slowly life returned to normal and Ash started saving again.

Soon enough Ash found himself once again impatiently straining at the bank's miserable interest rate.

Then one day an old business associate approached him and offered him another chance to soar with the eagles. Ash weakened.

Charles was an investment guru and offered him an annual 25 per cent return on his investment, plus the return of his principal after four years. Four years to double his money! This was the chance Ash was looking for. Ash did the math and checked the references. They all sang off the same song-sheet. The investment seemed sound. Once again he took the bait.

Doubt started to visit Ash when he overheard some of the customers referring to Charles in loud voices, but he'd received his first two interest payments in good order and he remained confident. He'd called Charles to double check, but Charles spoke with reassurance and promised to get back to him with more data.

Soon after, on his way to work, he bought the morning newspaper. To his horror he saw Charles splashed across the front page. It wasn't good news.
Once more Ash felt the earth crack open under his feet and he felt himself falling, falling, falling - slowly backward into a deep dark hole. Once again the abyss had opened up and claimed his life.

Ash sat, perched on the edge of the breakwater, trying to figure out what he was going to do about this new stuff-up. The drizzle blended with his salty tears. Should he simply jump? He realized that without TK's guidance he was going nowhere.

He sat there, crumpled, in defeat. He surrendered.

Unbeknown to Ash, Destiny was also present. She took one look at her pupil and had to admit that he was indeed thoroughly miserable. Maybe this time he had learned how to appreciate the gifts of wealth.

Maybe it was time to give him another chance.

Ash watched the fisherman reel in a fish, unhook it, and drop it into the catch bucket. Then he re-baited the hook and cast it back into the water. Ash looked morosely at the lonely fish swimming around inside the catch bucket. He realized that he had a lot in common with that fish, trapped in a bucket-full of water.

The stupid fish, he realized, swallows the bait whole and gets caught, while the cautious fish nibbles the bait from the hook and escapes with a full belly. Ash took the lesson. He accepted that once again he'd been hooked by greed.

What was the secret of the Money Fountain? TK had said it would make money work for you – and not you for it. But how? Ash had to find out.

He prayed. There seemed little else to do, other than to jump. Seated on the cold stonework in the drizzle, he prayed, and asked that TK be returned to him.

He didn't want the big swim. He didn't want to leap into the cold green sea and end his life. His resolve, his survival instinct, returned. This time, he said to himself, he'd be wise about his money.

There was only one road ahead – to take it on the chin, and start again. He resolved to be more conservative with his savings. He would no longer seek shortcuts to financial wealth. His days of soaring with the eagles were over. He was humbled.

It was still raining when he stood up and made his way back to his car - the hood of his jacket pulled tightly over his head.

"Ash?"

He didn't hear.

"Ash!" the voice called again, louder.

Ash was lost in his thoughts and didn't hear the pattering of feet running up behind him. Neither did he hear the way they slowed down as they came closer.

A hand touched his forearm.

"Ash?"

Ash turned and looked into the man's face.

"TK?"

"Yes."

"TK!"

"Ash. What's wrong?"

"TK! Is it really you?" Ash grabbed both of TK's hands in his.

"None other."

Ash's knees buckled. He sank to the ground in surrender - defeated, subdued, submitting.

Exactly the way that Destiny wanted him.

Chapter 5. Dr. Swan

Ash had to climb a long, steep hill to reach Dr. Swan's home.

It was so long and steep that when he got to the top of the hill he needed a few minutes to slow his heart rate, mop his brow and make himself presentable.

There was a button next to the heavy wooden door. Ash pressed it.

A minute passed. Two minutes. Then Ash heard a key turning in the lock. The door, still chained, opened a crack. A pair of cautious eyes peeped out.

"Can I help you?"

"Good morning Dr Swan."

"And you are?" The voice sounded dignified but guarded.

"TK's friend. Ash."

"What do you want?"

"TK said he'd made an appointment for me."

"I don't recall that."

"Are you Dr Swan?"

"Yes."

"Well then, there can't be a mistake," said Ash.

"Of course there's no mistake," said Dr Swan. "It's my day off, so I definitely don't have any appointments scheduled." He paused and studied Ash. "But I do have a few moments to spare. You said TK sent you?"

"Yes."

"Please wait."

The door closed and Ash heard the sound of a heavy chain being moved. The door opened halfway to reveal a tall grey-haired gentleman, warily studying him. Then, standing back, Dr Swan opened the door wide. "Please come in."

"Thank you," said Ash, stepping into a cool courtyard.

Dr. Swan was built like a long-distance runner: tall and lean, with long athletic legs and a light upper body. His bold Roman nose seemed designed to part the air as it streamed over his handsome face. He formed his words as an English gentleman would, and his actions told of a cautious man. Ash placed him at a healthy sixty-five.

Dr. Swan closed the door with a solid shove, turned the key, and then tried the handle - making doubly sure the latch had caught. Then he turned and gestured with his hand. "Please come through."

They walked down a short pathway which led past a pond with a fountain and large goldfish gulping air. The front door was open and Ash stepped into a lobby with coat racks, a hat stand and shelves of books.

"Would you like a cup of tea?" asked Dr Swan.

"Thank you," said Ash.

"How do you take it?"

"Strong with milk and one sugar, please."

"Coming up," said Dr. Swan. "Please make yourself comfortable in the lounge while I get the tea. If my daughter comes down - please ignore her."

Before Ash could answer, Dr. Swan disappeared, leaving him alone.
He turned to take in the view. Wow! Set on the slopes of Table Mountain, Dr. Swan's home looked east across the Cape Flats to the distant Hottentots' Holland mountains, where the sun rose.

The lounge and dining area faced a wall of glass; double doors led onto a polished marble patio which extended across a sprawling lawn toward a sparking swimming pool at the far side of the garden.

Dr Swan's home was both refined and modern, while the furnishings reflected a strong colonial-era influence. The living area was decorated in shades of soft white and dark green. It was warm and smelt of sandalwood with a hint of orange.

A bright painting of a dark-skinned man wearing a fez hung above the dining table. Though Ash did not know it this was an original Irma Stern. He liked the colors.

A painting of Table Mountain hung in the lounge. Ash admired the quality of the light in this painting, though he did not know that it was by South Africa's early landscape artist Thomas Baines. Soft background music filled the room with peace. Ash liked that as well, but once again he had no idea that it was Cavatina, a medley of tranquil classical Spanish guitar pieces.

Just at that moment Dr. Swan's daughter swept down the stairs in her bikini - her sarong trailing behind her like a veil.

She walked straight past Ash without even acknowledging him. Biff - take that.

Ash felt it.

Ash sniffed the air. He noticed that Ms. Swan left a sweet-scented trail behind her. He detected a delicate aroma of cocoa butter and a touch of rose. Above that there was something which he couldn't quite put his nose to.

Then Ms. Swan made her way across the lawn toward the deck chair at the edge of the pool – where she sank down and arranged the sarong around her long-tanned legs.

It was at this point that Ash realized she was perfectly aware of his presence - and that she was playing a game with him.

'Careful, little fish - you've been caught before.'

Ash heard the warning as he had heard previous warnings, deep inside his mind.

But now Ash had grown up, and he was wiser. His experience at the University of Hard Knocks had taught him to spot trouble, and this time he was able to recognize the siren.

"I see you," said Ash. Then he turned away from the window, and smiled, and his smile grew into a chuckle - a warm hearty chuckle, like the kind that one enjoys with good friends.

"What's so funny?" asked Dr. Swan. He'd approached unnoticed carrying a tray with the tea things.

"Er, your home's fantastic, Dr. Swan," stammered Ash.

"Please be seated," said Dr. Swan - aware that Ash had sidestepped his question.

"Thank you," said Ash as he struggled to lower himself onto the green leather couch without spilling his tea.

He suddenly felt like a little boy, and that was fair because it's exactly what he looked like.

A new pilgrim, thought Dr. Swan, *at the beginning of such an exciting journey.*

When he was certain that Ash was comfortable and wouldn't spill his tea, Dr. Swan speared him with a direct question.

"What were you laughing about?" Dr. Swan wasn't smiling now.

Ash stared at the floor for a few seconds, and then he looked up and met Dr. Swan's gaze. "I've been sidetracked by temptation before. These mistakes have cost me dearly. When you came in, I was laughing because temptation and I now recognize each other."

"Remarkable," said Dr. Swan, taking a sip from his cup. Then he changed the topic. "I spoke to TK while I was making the tea. He asked me to teach you about PYF."

"Pardon me…. PYF? I don't understand."

"Pay-Yourself-First - the first side to the Money Fountain."

"Oh yes!" said Ash. "Please excuse me - I've got some catching up to do."

"That's fine," said Dr. Swan. "So then – PYF. Why do you want to learn about it?"

"TK said that if I humbled myself and learned from my experience, you would teach me about the first side to the Money Fountain."

"Have you learned these arts?"

"Which arts?"

"Being humble, and recognizing temptation?"

"Yes – I believe I have," said Ash

"Mm…. Interesting," murmured Dr Swan, tapping his fingers on the armrest. "That's what TK said."

There was definitely something English about Dr Swan, and Ash liked it.

"But let's start at the beginning. Please tell me, what does wealth mean to you?"

"Before I met TK, in my old life, I thought wealth was just about money and good times," said Ash boldly. "But I've now come to understand that wealth is about health, love, family, environment, and contentment."

"Financial wealth," Ash continued, "offers security, but it's a means to an end. It isn't everything. It's an important part of life, but it doesn't mean that one should sacrifice one's life in its pursuit. True wealth is about contentment and love."

"Aha," said Dr. Swan. He congratulating Ash. "You are correct. That is the essence of wealth. Our purpose is to create financial security so that we can get on with enjoying the finer things in life. And we do that – don't we, Mr. Ash? - by creating a Money Fountain."

Ash felt a warm glow of reassurance.

"This will not happen overnight," warned Dr. Swan. "It will take you at least twenty-five years, but after that you will be financially stable and independent. However - a Money Fountain will only succeed if you follow the rules. Are you with me?"

"I am," confirmed Ash.

"When I say 'follow the rules'," said Dr. Swan seriously, "I don't mean follow them a little bit and cut some corners here and there. You need to follow the rules to the last letter. Is that understood?"

Ash swallowed and nodded. He was beginning to realize that the Fellowship was no Mickey Mouse affair.

"My purpose," said Dr. Swan, "is to explain to you the operating system of the first and most important side of the triangle - PYF. I will explain each point and how to implement it in sequence. You'd best take notes."

"And, please remember, if you don't implement each point in the correct sequence your Money Fountain will not function. Understood?"

Ash nodded. This sounded serious, which indeed it was.

"There are no shortcuts," warned Dr. Swan again - sternly. "If you commit to the program, after twenty-five years you will have gained financial independence. You will be free. This is a gift you can leave to your children."

"I understand," said Ash, reflecting on his recent lessons on shortcuts and gift horses.

"If I understand TK correctly," said Dr Swan, "you have a job and it sounds as if you are enjoying this, and you have managed to save part of your income."

"And lost it," confessed Ash. "Twice."

"None the less," said Dr. Swan, "you've done well. Don't underestimate the significance of your achievements. You are on the way to becoming financially independent."

"Thank you," said Ash, feeling a little more confident. "But I'm frustrated. The bank's interest rate is low and I don't know who to trust with my savings to get a better return on them."

"I understand the pressing nature of your question," said Dr. Swan. "But, first things first. Big Julius and Mrs. Blumkin will explain how and what to do with your money. Our present purpose is to discuss the PYF principle, and there's quite a bit that goes into the finer details. My commitment to you is to explain these."

"I'm in your debt."

"We will see about that," said Dr. Swan, clearing his throat with a polite cough. "It is possible," he began, "to turn $1 into $5 625 in twenty-five years. All you need is commitment, patience and time. Then, after twenty-five years, your wealth will continue to grow exponentially."

Twenty-five years? Ash reflected. That was a big chunk of time, but then all of his get-rich-quick schemes had flopped. He resolved to learn all he could from the Fellowship and decided then and there to commit himself to the program.

"In the beginning," continued Dr. Swan, "you won't have much spare cash. But after twenty-five years your Money Fountain will be flowing strongly. You will be set for a comfortable life and retirement. And your children will be free."

"Free?" asked Ash.

"Yes. Free. Your children will go to work for fun – for the pleasure of it, not for mere survival."
Dr. Swan took a sip of tea, sat back in his armchair and crossed his legs.

"The first secret of the Money Fountain is to PYF - pay yourself first."

"You've said so," replied Ash, "but what does that mean? I get paid once a month and that's it."

"But is all that money yours to keep?"

"Well, yes," said Ash. "It's mine, after all. I earn it."

"You are wrong," replied Dr Swan. "It isn't all your own. Your income is the money that your employer agreed to pay you when you started work. However, not all of that money is yours."

"I don't get it," said Ash. He didn't like the message.

"Very well," said Dr. Swan. "Let me explain. Before your salary is deposited into your bank account you have to pay tax. This is deducted by your employer before you get paid – and then paid directly to the taxman."

"Yes."

"So the Government takes the first bite, and every time you go shopping or put fuel into your car, the Government takes another bite. Value-Added Tax. Are you with me?

Ash nodded, but he was feeling a little bit resentful about all this. He took a sip of tea and refocused.

"So, as you now know, not all your money is yours to keep. There are a lot of other demands on your income as well."

"Given these taxes and the other demands, it is very difficult to save. And unless you have a savings plan your Money Fountain won't work."

Ash heard the warning. He swallowed hard.

"You understand then that there's a difference between your income, or what you get paid, and your take-home pay?"

He nodded. Dr. Swan continued.

"Now this is important. Your take-home pay is the money you have left after the Government has taken its first bite - the income tax on your wage."

Ash nodded again. That much was obvious.

"Good. Now, the most important feature of a Money Fountain is to save 10% of your take-home pay and PYF. "

"PYF?"

"Pay-Yourself- First. I've already made that point, haven't I? Please be focused, Mr Ash. Now, this is the point - you will then invest that 10% in a facility that compounds the interest."

"What's that?" asked Ash.

"Mrs. Blumkin will guide you through that final aspect of creating a Money Fountain. But - first, - get a job. Ah – of course, you've said that you have one."

"Once you have secured a job, keep it. You do this by making work your friend. Enjoy the people you work with. Work hard, do more than is expected of you. Learn all you can about your job, make yourself attractive to other employers. You do this because …?"

Ash looked blank.

"You do this because your take-home-pay is the most vital ingredient to creating your Money Fountain."

"I understand, now," said Ash nodding.

"And this is where your PYF 10% is going to come from. This will be the source of your Money Fountain."

"Got it," said Ash enthusiastically.

"Very well," continued Dr. Swan. "Now you divide your take-home pay into ten equal portions …."

Ash listened.

"… and you pay the first 10% into a separate bank account, by stop order. And you do this before you pay anyone or anything else."

"Is that what you mean by Pay-Yourself-First?"

"Exactly," said Dr. Swan. "PYF - this 10% saving is vitally important. Fail here and you will remain enslaved."

"But how can I save 10% if I can't make ends meet on what I'm earning?"

"Well," retorted Dr. Swan, "the answer is obvious."

"What's that?"

"Cut your expenses."

"That makes sense," said Ash. "But I'll have to do without some things."

"Exactly," confirmed Dr. Swan. "This is the next important lesson - learn the difference between essential and desirable spending. So, what is essential in your life?"

"Well - I need food, clothes, somewhere to live, and money to get to work."

"That's about it," confirmed Dr. Swan again.

"Now a nice car, or a nice big TV or expensive dinners out – those are desires, not essential items. So, the first thing you need to do is make a list of your essential items, and make that fit into 9/10ths of your take-home pay. "

"Understood," said Ash – watching as his social life received a severe haircut.

"If you can manage to live on less than your 9/10th, then you have even more cash to save."

Ash felt this was do-able, and he relaxed a little – just before the next blow arrived.

"Now for the next hurdle," said Dr. Swan, clearing his throat again. "Debt - do you have any?"

"A little," acknowledged Ash.

"So, the next important lesson is to get yourself out of debt as quickly as possible."

"But how do I do that?" said Ash defensively.

"I was hoping you'd ask that," said Dr Swan enthusiastically. "It's a most important question and fortunately the answer's quite simple. You add all your debts into a single pile, and then divide it by the number of your debtors. Then, using another 2/10ths of your take-home pay, you pay them all equally from that 2/10ths budget."

"But if I'm already saving 1/10th, where will I find the other 2/10ths?"

"By cutting your costs even more," said Dr. Swan unsympathetically.

"Shoo," said Ash. He scratched his head. "That doesn't leave much cash for me."

"Well, who got themselves into debt in the first place?"

"I did," acknowledged Ash.

"I was hoping you'd say that too," said Dr. Swan smiling.

"Since you created the debt you have to repay it - and you need to do this as quickly as possible. Using the 2/10ths formula has other benefits."

"What are those?

"Once you have paid off your debts the 2/10ths becomes available for greater savings, and this will dramatically speed up the flow of your Money Fountain. "And," said Dr. Swan raising his forefinger in the air, "your debtors will have more respect for you and want to lend you more."

"But why would I want to borrow more if I have to pay interest on the loan?"

"I was hoping you would say that as well," laughed Dr. Swan. "Avoid debt at all costs. So, if you have credit cards, cut them up now."

"Why?"

"Simple. The interest rates imposed by credit cards are very high. And the banks are putting your interest payments into their own Money Fountains - making them richer and you poorer. That's why."

Ash gasped as the penny dropped. "That's not good."

"Exactly!" confirmed Dr. Swan. "Remember now - when you start creating your own Money Fountain the first few years will be tough. But if you stick to the plan and work hard, it will get easier to save and to live off your 9/10ths."

Ash felt that he could do this.

"And because you are working hard and enjoying work you quickly forget about the limitations of your new budget – and then you get energized by your new routine and off you go. The point is to start PYF as soon as possible."

Ash reflected on this comment and nodded. Yes! He could feel a nice new energy rising inside himself.

"Remarkably - it doesn't matter how much or how little you earn. If you can save your 10% PYF you will become financially independent. It is simple math. All it takes is commitment and patience."

Ash nodded again, committing himself to follow the teaching.

"And don't buy a fancy car on credit."

"Why?"

"The purpose of a car is to get you from A to B, not to attract a mate."

Ash understood the downside of flashy cars.

Dr. Swan looked Ash straight in the eye. "Do you get my point?"

"Very clearly."

"Good. It's non-negotiable. Get this wrong and it's DCM."

"DCM?"

"Yes. DCM. Don't Come Monday."

Dr Swan cleared his throat and continued: "And DRB."

"DRB?" asked Ash again.

"Don't rent. Buy."

"Do you mean I should buy my own home?"

"Yes," said Dr Swan.

"But I will need to take a loan, and you've just advised against that."

"In this instance, and in this instance only, we advise you to borrow the money."

"Why?" asked Ash.

"If you rent all your life, when you retire you will have nothing to show for your efforts. Buy, even if you have to borrow to do so. Logic will prevail, and you can turn this loan to your advantage."

"How?" enquired Ash.

"First, buy a solid home in a modest area, and then pay off more than you have to. This will save you a fortune. But remember," said Dr. Swan raising a stern finger again, "always PYF."

Ash was still not completely sure how taking a loan to buy a house could work for him.

"Many people who live in expensive houses don't actually own them," said Dr. Swan, chuckling to himself. "The lending agency owns them. The highest percentage of people who actually own their own homes live in the less costly areas."

Then he gazed into the distance and thought for a while. "There's a lovely story about Elvis Presley," he said, chuckling again.

"Would you like to hear it?"

"Very much," said Ash. He liked Elvis Presley's music.

"When Elvis first moved into Graceland the neighbors weren't at all thrilled and they wanted him to move on. So they called a neighborhood meeting at which they hoped to draw up a petition – demanding that Elvis move. But when the meeting opened, the bank manager stood up and reminded them that Elvis was the only one who had actually paid for his house. The meeting closed very quickly after that."

Ash laughed. He understood.

"The point is that in the rich areas the bank owns most of the houses. This isn't wealth. It looks like wealth but it's just a façade, a boost for the ego. In truth, these people are slaves who work to pay the interest on their loans, and thereby work to provide the source for the lender's Money Fountain. The higher your expenses, the harder you have to work. Get it?"

Ash got it.

"When you own your home you are wealthy, and it doesn't matter where that home is. You are wealthy. Your cost of living drops. So when it comes to buying a home, it is wise to buy in a modest area. And as I said, in this case it is okay to borrow the money, but pay back more than you need to. In this instance, and this instance alone, debt can work for you."

Ash pictured a modest house in his mind as Dr Swan continued:

"Security is also an integral part of the operating system of Paying Yourself First."

Ash pictured his modest house with burglar bars on the windows, but Dr. Swan dispelled that image:

"Wealth needs protection. Wealth clings to protection. So take out life insurance and make a will."

Ash looked bewildered. Dr. Swan, noticing this, stared into the distance for a while, trying to conjure up a suitable example to illustrate the importance of his point about protection. Finally, he settled on the example of walls:

"In ancient times," spoke Dr. Swan, "walls offered good insurance from danger and marauding armies. Take Babylon for example."

"Babylon?"

"Yes. Babylon. It was a large city in the Middle East built on a fertile plain between two rivers. It wasn't on a trade route, it didn't have mountains with minerals to be mined, it didn't have a port for shipping, or forests for timber, and yet it was fabled for its wealth, and for its lush Hanging Gardens. How come?"

"I have no idea," said Ash.

"All that Babylon had going for it was water, good soil, and the labor of its citizens. The farmers made profits and paid taxes, which the city elders invested in building big strong walls – walls that offered protection from attack. When invading armies did attack, the farmers simply retreated behind their walls and waited for the attackers to run out of steam. Eventually, unable to breach the walls and because armies are expensive to maintain, the invaders packed up and went home. When the coast was clear, the farmers emerged, restored their lands, and continued producing. In this way Babylon's walls were their insurance and the secret to their success. In the same way, you need to use insurance to protect your family's future and the fruits of your labor."

Journal entry

How to turn $1 into $5,625 in 25 years. PYF : Pay Yourself First - no shortcuts.

Get a job, work hard, make work your friend, enjoy the people you work with, learn everything there is to learn about the job, make yourself attractive to other employers.

Most important : don't wait to grow income before starting to save 10%. Start saving now – over time, your salary will grow.

Save 10% of take-home pay - the difference between income and take-home pay.

Establish difference between essential and desirable expenditure - set a new budget that fits 9/10 of take-home pay.

Pay off debts using 2/10th of take-home pay – that leaves 7/10ths to live on. Ouch! But I created the debt and only I can get out of it, and as quickly as possible.

Don't get into more debt… return credit cards asap… they're really debt cards. What a grand idea.

Buy own home in a modest area… cheaper… I agree.

Chapter 6. Fish Hoek Beach

The venue that TK had chosen for Ash's lesson on protection was the outdoor restaurant on Fish Hoek beach – which was famous for all the wrong reasons.

A Great White shark patrolled the shore and had already devoured a few swimmers. Eerily, the beast always left a calling card: sometimes a bathing cap, sometimes a pair of goggles, and sometimes a limb.

Much to the public's horror, not only was the shark comfortable dining in broad daylight, it was also happy cruising the shallows just beyond the breakers, where bathers could see it.

Once again, making his way to the beach, Ash had to cross the railway tracks, but this time depression did not accompany him. And he was early - because he had a new interest, a new enthusiasm about what could be possible.

The waitress took his coffee order.

Ash chose to sit outside, at one of the brightly colored tables under the umbrellas and palm trees. From his seat he had a view across the bay to the distant Hottentots Holland Mountains, where the sun rose.

The sun was bright, and only a few puffy clouds drifted across the sky. The beach was bustling with many young mothers who had brought their children to enjoy the fine weather. While there were many people on the beach, Ash noticed that only a few ventured into the water. And none of them ventured deeper than their knees. When a big wave approached, the bathers quickly retreated.

His coffee arrived, and Ash studied it. He noted that the foam had bubbles and didn't support the weight of the sugar. The milk had obviously been heated to more than 145°F.

Ash wondered about TK's preference for outdoor eating establishments - they all seemed so down-market, especially when it came to cappuccino.

The train whistle brought Ash back to the moment, and when he looked up TK was standing in front of him. Ash laughed:

"What is it with you?" he asked as TK seated himself. "The coffee here is terrible."

TK, appreciating Ash's observation, smiled. "I love the outdoors. It's our greatest wealth, and it's meant to be enjoyed. True wealth is to be found in your environment, not in your pocket. Or the quality of the coffee foam."

The waitress approached the table and TK ordered a cappuccino.

"We are meeting today," he began, "because Dr Swan reported that you didn't understand the protection aspect of the Money Fountain. This session will focus on protection and security, and I will fill in those gaps for you, but you will need to see professionals when you come to implement the process."

"Understood," said Ash nodding.

"Life insurance and wills are two essential aspects of the Money Fountain. Like the walls of Babylon, they offer you protection and security - both of which are needed to ensure the flow of a Money Fountain. Without these yours efforts and gains could well be wasted."

Again Ash nodded. The warning seemed important and he knew that it was time to stop procrastinating. He knew all about waste.

"When you start on the road to creating wealth you need to ensure that your gains are secured," said TK firmly. "You may not always need life insurance, but you will always need a will." He stared hard at Ash.

"Protection," continued TK, "comes in the form of different insurances that one needs at different times in one's life."

"When you have a young family and a new home, you need to insure your life and your debts. These priorities will change in your mid-life and retirement. Protecting your family is a structured program, and, as you will see, it's an essential element of the ongoing functioning of your Money Fountain. Remember, the true beneficiaries of your Money Fountain will be your children and grandchildren."

"You mean my Money Fountain is a gift that I will leave to them?"

"Yes," confirmed TK. "Therefore, the ultimate rationale behind your investment and insurance must be your will."

"What is a will?"

"A will determines how your assets will be distributed when you cross over."

Ash swallowed deeply – he feared the unknown.

"This event is inevitable," said TK seriously. "And it could happen at any moment. You never know when the bell will toll for you, so why not plan for it while you can?"

Ash agreed. Push had come to shove.

At this juncture TK's coffee arrived. He looked at it critically. Then he shrugged and grinned. "The foam's awful, but it's a beautiful day and we are alive. Cheers, young man. Here's to your Money Fountain!"

"Thank you," said Ash raising his cappuccino. "But - I wonder why outdoor establishments always seem to produce such substandard fare."

"I don't know," said TK. "Maybe it's a message about priorities. What is really important? Coffee is coffee - some good, some bad."

"But look over there," he said, pointing to the mothers on the beach. "There's love. That, Ash, is what life is all about – love; and protection."

Ash understood. He liked TK's point. TK continued.

"Making a will gives you great peace of mind. It removes that nagging feeling of 'what if' from the equation."

"Once you've drawn up a will and resolved your insurance, you'll feel much more confident and secure, and this will encourage good luck to your side." TK took a sip of his coffee. "But if you die without a will, you are considered intestate."

"What's that?" interrupted Ash.

TK sighed and ran his fingers through his hair as he realized the extent of the task that lay before him.

"Intestate means that you've died without leaving a will. In that case the state freezes your assets and the courts wind up your estate. This is a protracted and expensive process. It will take years, and it will cost a fortune," said TK. He wore an ominous frown. "Your debts will be settled first, and any legal fees related to a court case will be paid before your family sees a cent."
"The court will then distribute the remaining monies according to a set of rules. And - unfortunately - your family will be last in the queue. They will be the biggest losers."

"Why?" asked Ash.

"Well. Lawyers charge by the hour. And once a settlement is finalized they won't be able to charge any more fees. So why should they rush to settle? It pays then to not find a solution."

"Oh," said Ash. He thought about it. "I guess that makes sense."

"To put it plainly, not having a will is the stupidest avoidable mistake – but a lot of folk make that mistake."

TK made an excellent point. He, Ash, was unprotected, and now he realized how short-sighted this was.

"And to make matters even worse – as your debts and lawyers' fees are paid first your family loses the lump sum that is paid out by life insurance. This money could have been invested and your debts paid from the dividends."

"In the same way that debtors are paid out of two-tenths of income?" asked Ash.

"Exactly," confirmed TK. "If they had retained the lump sum they could have settled the debt out of dividend payments and retained the principal."

Ash swallowed. He was staring into the harsh looking glass of reality.

"Not making a will is short-sighted and silly. Besides, it only takes a few hours to draw one up. But be warned, while the service is free there are hidden costs and catches. I will come to those."

Ash nodded. "I'm getting it," he said.

"Even if you're in prime health, you've got no way of knowing when your number's up."

"Point taken, said Ash. "I'll see to it immediately."

"So let me explain the finer points of a will. Are you ready?"

A sudden breeze rustled the palms and a cloud stole the sunlight, but Ash remained focused.

"In your will you will nominate your beneficiaries, and set the conditions as to how your assets will be managed. Your will is your opportunity to plan this."

"How do I make a will?" asked Ash.

"Well, it's best to consult a professional, but first enquire about the costs. This is crucial. Some lawyers and organizations will take up to 7% of your estate. They might also charge for meetings and phone calls. Believe you me, it all adds up very quickly. This is why they usually offer to draw up your will for free, and unless asked, don't mention the clause relating to their charges. Then again, if a bank draws up your will, they'll most probably nominate themselves as executors and they will take a fee for doing that. It's best to approach your family lawyer and confirm a locked-off fee."

"There are a couple of other basics about a will. It must be signed and dated by you, the testator, and witnessed by at least two competent witnesses, neither of whom can be beneficiaries."

"What is a testator?"

"The testator is you, the person who writes and signs the will. Testate means having left a legally valid will."

The waitress interrupted TK to take their orders for food. Neither of them was sure, and they asked her to come back later.

More clouds had gathered in the sky, stealing away yet more of the sun.

TK continued: "But before you go and see your lawyer, map out what your estate consists of. That means you need to list your assets and your liabilities or what you owe your debtors, who the beneficiaries are, how your assets are to be distributed, and finally, you need to nominate your executors."

"Executors? What do they do?"

Again TK ran his hands through his hair. He gazed into the distance, seeking patience. When he found it, he sighed and continued.

"An executor's job is to make sure that your assets are distributed and managed according to your wishes. He or she is the person who is going to manage your family's future. You need to choose this person or persons, or institution, very carefully, and then nominate them in your will."

Ash scratched his head. This was more complex than he'd expected.

"When you nominate an executor, choose somebody who has your best interests at heart, like a family member or a friend. Your executor will have to attend quite a few meetings, so choose somebody you can trust and who lives nearby. An executor should also have money-management skills, and be honest and reliable."
"Just in case the person you nominate either can't, or is unwilling, to be your executor, you should nominate an alternative. But it's best to approach your nominees and seek their agreement - before you nominate them."

Ash nodded again.

"It's also a good idea to choose somebody who will probably outlive you," added TK with a faint smile. "For this reason an ageing parent might not be a great idea. This is why it's a good idea to nominate an alternative person as well."

"Got that," said Ash nodding.

"Part of an executor's job is to collect all the monies owed to you and pay your debts. He or she will also have to file all the proper tax documents, distribute your estate, and more. This is not an easy task, so think carefully about who you will entrust the responsibility to."

Ash nodded, regretting that he hadn't brought his notepad.

"Then - make sure your executors know where to find your will and your updated net-worth statement."

"A what?" asked Ash with alarm. His to-do list was growing by the minute, and these were complexities he'd never dreamed of.

TK laughed and took a sip of his coffee. Patience was now firmly seated beside him, and together they were prepared for the long haul.

"A net-worth statement records all your assets and liabilities or debts. When you subtract your debts from your assets you get your net worth."

TK studied Ash with a look of concern before continuing.

"Let us hope you own more than you owe. This is where life insurance is vital. Your will and insurance are vitally important if your family are to maintain the flow of your Money Fountain after you've gone."

It was now Ashes turn to run his fingers through his hair and sigh.

"If your will and net-worth statement are up to date, winding up your estate should be simple. This is for the benefit of your beneficiaries."

"These are the basic rules, and they are vital to the flow of your Money Fountain. Even though they sound simple, it is very important that you get them right."

"Right." said Ash, though he was still a little unsure. TK saw this.

"When we next meet, you need to give me proof that you've begun this process. Otherwise, this Fountain of Knowledge will dry up."

"Fair call," admitted Ash as he stared at the mountains in the distance. The gravity of his neglect was becoming abundantly clear.

"Not making a will is a needless stupid mistake. Do I have your word that you will see to this immediately?"

"Yes," said Ash.

"A few years ago," observed TK, "the council was going to install shark nets here. "But it hasn't happened yet. And their procrastination's cost a bather his life."

Ash got the point. He now understood the need for action, and TK was satisfied. He felt happy enough to continue with the lesson.

"So, now that you have a will let's focus on insurance and its benefits. Remember, your Money Fountain requires this security if it is to keep on flowing."

"Okay," agreed Ash. "But why do people buy life insurance?"

"So that when they cross over," responded TK patiently, "their families will have money to live on. But there are many more aspects to insurance. You will need different insurances at different times. When your Money Fountain begins to flow strongly, you might not need it, but while you're still enslaved it's vital."

Ash took a sip of his coffee which was cooling. He thought about his enslavement. His Money Fountain wasn't yet flowing strongly. He realized that he might still be enslaved.

"How do you work out how much money your family will need when you're gone?" prodded TK.

"I have absolutely no idea."

"When you die, your family won't be able to access the funds you leave them in your will until the estate's been settled. This takes time. And yet they'll be faced with immediate urgent costs. This is where life insurance kicks in. Your insurance must be able to pay off all your outstanding debts, such as your mortgage. It must cover funeral costs, the winding up of any business issues and, most important, provide interim living expenses for your family. Ideally this will mean a once-off lump sum that they can invest, and continue to enjoy the dividends."

Then TK leaned forward and looked Ash in the eye. "And please make sure that you include an additional 10% PYF – which will be invested in a compounding fund."

"And – when you start establishing how much cash your family will need, it is important to factor in inflation. This will be the number-one enemy of your beneficiaries."

"Why?"

"Inflation is the silent killer. Its eroding power is relentless. Because your beneficiaries will be living off the dividends of your savings their income will be reduced by creeping inflation. That's why it is important to instruct your executors to continue contributions to your Money Fountain."

"Right now," said TK taking a sip of his cold coffee, "we are still setting up the PYF side of your Money Fountain - and your will and insurance are vitally important parts of it. Fail here and your gains could well be lost."

Ash sighed. He had much to do. Every word that TK spoke revealed how unprepared he was to manage a Money Fountain. And this meant that he would not be able to enjoy its benefits.

"Sounds complicated, doesn't it?" conceded TK. "But once you've established your family's financial needs you can start approaching insurance companies about life insurance."

"Do your research and check out several policies before you choose one - and be sure to read the fine print before you sign any agreement. Ask as many questions as you need to, no matter how stupid they might seem. Enquire about fees and charges and get the figures in writing. If you don't understand, don't sign."

"I get it," said Ash. His coffee was cold but he took a sip anyway. The sun appeared from behind the clouds and brought warmth. Down on the beach the kids were having a great time. A boisterous group of boys were playing cricket.

"There are two types of insurance," continued TK. "Short and long term. Short-term covers things like cars, home mortgages, and the contents of your home – and the less you spend here the more money you've got that you can invest in your Money Fountain. Got it?"

Ash nodded.

"Long-term insurance, on the other hand, covers your family for the years to come after your death."

A tennis ball bounced past the table with two little boys chasing after it. They retrieved their ball and fled in a flurry of noise.

"The point is," said TK after settling down again, "that you only need life insurance when you have people that rely on your income. If you are single and don't have any kids, then you most probably won't need it. If you have debts like a home mortgage, then you do. If you are married and have children then you most definitely do."

"Do I need to insure my children?"

"No. They are liabilities."

"Liabilities! How?"

"Children are a liability because they cost you money. If they cross over, they will leave a massive emotional gap in your life, but your expenses will drop."

"Not nice," said Ash.

"But true," retorted TK. "In the broader sense of the word, a liability is a debt for which you are responsible - so in a way a child is a liability because you have an obligation to finance their education and lifestyle until they are independent. And this is why you need life insurance."

"Is my wife a liability?"

"If a spouse does not work, you could see it that way. But if she is a home-maker, rearing your family, she is an asset and you may want to insure her life. For instance, if your wife suddenly crosses over, you, the surviving partner, are going to have to cope with a lot more than grief at her sudden departure. There are millions of things house mums do that are unseen and unappreciated. So, in the ideal world, you will want to insure your wife's life for the total of your combined debts, including the mortgage on your house. This is a good idea because a debt-free balance sheet greatly reduces the stress on a suddenly single parent. There will be other costs like funeral expenses, day care, and babysitters. The surviving parent is going to need more money than you suspect - so plan for the event."

Ash was going pale.

"Put some more sugar in your coffee," directed TK.

"Why?"

"You're losing focus!"

TK waited while Ash poured another sachet of sugar into his cold coffee and stirred it. He took a sip and his color returned.
TK continued.

"Your life insurance should also make provision for the event that both you and your partner cross over within a short space of each other - leaving your child an orphan."

"What a horrid thought."

"I agree," said TK. "It might sound morbid at this moment, but believe me, your survivors will be much more confident when they are standing next to your coffin if they know that you've been brave enough to face these issues - and prepare for them in advance."

"I suppose so," said Ash, watching the children playing on the beach. They'd given up cricket and were now making mud pies at the water's edge. Then they started a mud fight - hurling the pies at each other. A mother ran down and scolded them, putting a swift end to the game. The boys objected loudly but to no avail. The mother was soon seen packing up.

As Ash watched this family enjoying its day on the beach he realized just how important it was to have a will and life insurance.

Journal entry.

Fish Hoek Beach, sharks, crap coffee. Thank you TK.

Will sets out how my assets will be distributed. Intestate = dying without a will. NOT GOOD. State resolves my will…will pay debts and lawyers' fees first…family gets what is left and loses control over lump sum, which could have been used to pay debts using the 2/10 formula.

Will—must consult a professional. NOTE: See charges and costs. Executors implement provisions in the will, pay all taxes, etc. Executors need to be honest, reliable, live close by, and be good with money. Nominate an alternative. Net-worth statement lists assets and debts (value = total assets less debts). Tell executors where will is and lodge net-worth statement with it. Good idea! Executors collect all monies owed and pay debt. IMPORTANT: Debts can be settled from 2/10.

Life insurance - must cover debts and maintain family. Add 10% for future investments and component for inflation, banking fees, and costs.

Short and long term insurance: short-term covers mortgage and cars. Long-term covers life insurance…maybe Money Fountain covers this? Check with TK. Don't insure kids; have a plan in case both parents are killed together (awful thought).

Life insurance: two types. Cash value insures life with forced saving component. Might not be necessary if I am investing 10 % in Money Fountain? Term insurance - cover will cease when policy matures, company might load new fees. Seek a policy that addresses this.

Plan for retirement. TK suggests Money Fountain might do the trick…am not so sure; many questions remain.

Chapter 7. Big Julius

Having planned his journey and bought the ticket Ash found himself on a bus traveling through the rolling green hills of the Eastern Cape - heading for Coffee Bay.

It wasn't an air-conditioned luxury bus, but it was a warm, fun bus.

Destiny found Ash tucked in amongst some old women and men, children, sacks of corn, chickens, two goats and a piglet. It smelt like Africa and Ash liked it.

They spent the morning driving over and around hills, passing small villages of mud and thatch-roofed huts, small cultivated fields, and roaming cattle.

The bus occasionally swerved to miss the bigger potholes, but most of the time the driver just crashed straight through and hurried along.
Now and then the bus drew up and somebody got on or off, but never at a bus stop. There were no fences, and the dogs didn't bother to chase the bus.

At midday the bus arrived at a trading store which was perched on the edge of an escarpment. From his window Ash could see over the wooded escarpment and down to the coast. On the shoreline, far below, was a rocky feature called the Hole-in-the-Wall. Ash had read about it and recognized the spur of rock rising straight out of the ocean. It was cut off from the land, and stood in the waves like a stubborn slice of toast. Its top was crowned with dense bush. In the center of the massive grey stone base was a large hole worn through by the sea. At high tide the waves burst through the hole with spectacular violence.

Without fanfare the bus driver closed the doors and drove on, plunging into the forest. In the early afternoon the bus arrived in Coffee Bay.

Ash was the last person to get off at the last stop - the beach - and the first person he met was a young herd boy. There were cows lazing on the beach and the herd boy was watching over them. TK had told Ash that this was the person who would take him to Big Julius.

"Hello," said Ash approaching the herd boy. "I'm looking for Big Julius. Do you know where I can find him?"

"Sure," said the boy.

"Can you take me to him?"

"Sure," said the boy again. "But it's too late to go now. I can take you tomorrow if you like. We must walk. Okay?"

"How far is it?" asked Ash.

"A long way."

"What's your name?"

"Vuyo."

"How much will you charge to take me to Big Julius?"

"One hundred rand."

"Okay," said Ash. "But where can I stay tonight?"

"The hotel over there," said Vuyo pointing at a big white building above the beach. "I will meet you at this place here at sunrise tomorrow morning. Bring a hat."

The first pink blush of the approaching dawn found Ash standing on the beach, looking out to sea. He felt at peace with himself and he closed his eyes in a thankful prayer. When he opened his eyes Vuyo was standing in front of him.

"It's sunrise," said Vuyo. "We go. Yes?"

"Good morning," said Ash.

"You pay me now," said Vuyo without ceremony, holding out both hands.

Ash handed over a new one-hundred-rand note with the face of Madiba on it.

"When will we get there?"

"When the sun is there," said Vuyo pointing to a position in the sky which Ash estimated to be three in the afternoon. Then Vuyo turned and started walking.

Ash grabbed his day pack and hurried after Vuyo, who set a cracking pace. The path led to the end of the beach and then it climbed over a hill. From the crest it plunged down into a milkwood forest and re-emerged on another beach which was strewn with boulders.

A short way off the coast stood the majestic Hole-in-the-Wall.

Waves crashed through the hole and into a large pool in front of its mouth. There was a river of fresh water that flowed down from the escarpment and into the pool. It looked like a great place for a swim.

"We cross here," said Vuyo pointing to a narrow sand bar that ran just beneath the water level. Then he pointed to the sea beyond the sand bar: "Over there - sharks."

Ash, struggling to take off his shoes, smiled to himself. Bare-foot at last. He now realized just how much of the country boy still lived in him.

He put his trainers into his pack, shouldered it, and waded across the sand bar. When he emerged from the pool Vuyo was waiting for him. But Vuyo didn't hang around for him to put his shoes on. Turning, the herd boy followed a path that ran along the riverbank.

They followed the path for half an hour and then came to a fork. One path continued along the riverbank - the other led into the forest. Vuyo took that, heading into the trees.

Twisting around the contours of hills, the path climbed steadily all morning. There were breaks in the forest with small compounds of mud and thatch huts set in fields of cultivated corn.

Unseen voices called out, and though Ash could not understand what was being said, Vuyo always responded with something that included the words Big Julius.

Vuyo walked quickly and seldom waited for Ash. Late in the morning, while climbing along the edge of a precipice, they came to another break in the trees. Across the valley Ash saw a waterfall plunge over the edge of the escarpment and disappear into the thick forest far below. He wanted to pause and take it in, but Vuyo had little time for the view. He kept up his cracking pace while Ash struggled to keep up. They continued for another two hours and then emerged on a rock platform high above the forest.

"We take a break here," said Vuyo.

Ash was grateful. He was parched. He scratched in his pack and brought out two bottles of water, one of which he gave to Vuyo. Then he produced a packet of sandwiches that the hotel had made for him.

He gave half to Vuyo.

Ash noticed that every time he handed Vuyo a gift, the herd boy clapped his wrists together twice and then accepted the gift with both hands, bowed his head, and said "Enkosi".

After lunch the path continued to climb through the forest. Late in the afternoon, they emerged below a cluster of huts in a clearing on the edge of a small plateau.

"Big Julius lives here," said Vuyo. "I am going now."

"What do you mean? How will I get back?"

"They will sort it out," said Vuyo, raising his hand in farewell.

"Thank you my friend," said Ash. "Goodbye."

But he spoke to the wind. Vuyo had already melted into the forest.

Alone, Ash turned to climb the last few steps. He had been walking and climbing for the best part of eight hours. He was exhausted and sweaty and his knees ached.

He took a deep breath and ascended the final steps. At the top of these, he emerged into a compound with five mud huts. They were painted a rich chocolate brown and set in a semicircle around a central courtyard which was surrounded by a low retaining wall.

A large mango tree grew in the center of the courtyard with a half circle of benches set under its shade.
Ash imagined that this was the tree where the elders gathered for their indaba, their tribal council.

There was an open cooking fire above which a three-legged pot bubbled. The wood-smoke drifted across the courtyard. It smelt of Africa and, once again, it filled Ash with a sense of belonging.

"Hello," he called out, "is anybody home?"

Nobody answered. Ash waited a few moments and then called again.

"Wait!" a voice answered, but Ash couldn't tell where it came from.

The door of the hut next to the cooking fire opened and a very sleepy bare-chested maiden emerged, rubbing her eyes and yawning.

"Hello," said Ash trying to ignore her breasts. He spoke brightly and tried to cover his awkwardness. "I've come to see Big Julius."

"Who?" responded the girl, studying him with an air of sleepy confusion.

"Big Julius."

"No," she said, shaking her head. "No Big Julius here."

"What do you mean?"

"No Big Julius here."

"I don't understand. There must be a mistake. I've just walked the whole way from Coffee Bay to see Big Julius and you tell me there's no Big Julius?"

"Sorry." She looked about her. "Big Julius? I don't know him."

"Vuyo brought me all the way here to see him!" Ash felt sudden panic and exasperation.

The young lady looked at Ash with suspicion.

"Did you pay Vuyo?"

"Yes."

"Nah," she laughed. "You got taken."

After the long walk Ash felt his blood pressure rising.

"Vuyo does this all the time," continued the young lady. "We have many visitors like you. I don't know why."

"I don't believe you," said Ash feeling the frustration and anger well up inside him. Strong words were not far away.

"Look here," he demanded. "Don't you know Big Julius?"

"Hayi. No. Sorry. If you've walked the whole way and Vuyo has taken your money, then I am sorry for you. Yho, that Vuyo," she added, shaking her head. "He is trouble."

Just as Ash was about to explode, a new voice called out and entered the fray.

"Molly! Molly! Stop that immediately."

Ash hit the bottom of the rabbit hole with a bump and looked around.

Up on the crest of the hill stood an elderly dark-skinned man in a white linen suit. He was a short, thin man with grey hair and round spectacles and he walked with the aid of a stick. He made his way gingerly down the slope. He entered the courtyard and approached Ash.

"Are you Ash?"

"Yes," said Ash.

"TK said you might arrive today."

"Are you Big Julius?"

"Yes and no," said the old man smiling.

"Don't believe him!" shouted the girl. "He always pretends to be Big Julius!"

The old man interrupted her. "Let me start at the beginning. First, I apologize about Molly. She gets a kick out of watching visitors' faces."

"Don't believe him!" shouted Molly again. "He always does this."

"Tula, Molly!" shouted the old man. "I am Big Julius, and I am not. Big Julius is a nickname. As you can see I'm not very big." He chuckled warmly. "But, if you like, you can call me Julius."

Soon enough Ash found himself freshly showered and standing alone in a large room. This had a magnificent view over the escarpment, the forest, and the ocean. Ash noted the polished wooden desk with a laptop and mobile phone.

"Do you like the view?" asked Big Julius. He had entered silently, behind Ash.

"Yes, indeed. It's wonderful."

"Beats living in the city. Would you like a gin and tonic?"

"No thank you," replied Ash "I don't touch alcohol."

"Each to his own," said Big Julius. "What can I get you?"

"A cup of tea would be great."

Julius took Ash by the arm and led him to an olive-green leather couch which was scattered with white cushions. The colors reminded Ash of Dr Swan's lounge.

"I'm pleased you like my set-up," said Julius. "Do you know - we're entirely off grid. We work off solar power, biogas and wind. But the wind's not that consistent here, so we depend mostly on solar and biogas."

"That's impressive."

"Thank you," said Big Julius. He smiled. "I enjoy being in nature. It's much more peaceful than living in the city. I don't think I could live there anymore. And with modern technology I can run my business from here just as if I was in the city."

Ash liked the music that was playing on the CD though he didn't know that the mellow crooning voice was that of Chet Baker. The lyrics sounded something like 'everything happens to me'.

When Ash was comfortable Big Julius pressed a buzzer next to him. "Molly, please bring Mr Ash a cup of tea. I'll have my usual."

"Isn't it a bit early?" asked Molly's voice over the intercom.

"That will be all, thank you," said Big Julius firmly. He turned to Ash: "I believe you've met with Dr. Swan?"

"Yes."

"Nice chap. How did that go?"

"Well, thank you," said Ash glancing around him. Still adjusting to his new environment.

"Tell me what you talked about."

"Dr. Swan revealed the PYF operating mechanism of the Money Fountain. Then I met with TK and he taught me about protection."

"You mean wills and life insurance?"

"Yes," said Ash. "And he said that you would teach me about the second side of the Money Fountain - the Magic Penny."

At this moment Molly arrived with the tea and a drink for Big Julius. Much to Ash's relief Molly was now properly dressed. She gave Ash his tea, stood back, and looked him directly in the eye. Then she winked and smiled.

"You look much more comfortable now, Mr. Ash," she said. "Did you enjoy your shower?"

"Thank you," said Ash cautiously. He wasn't certain if he trusted Molly.

"One and a half sugars?"

"Thank you."

"Loser," said Molly with a smile. So saying, she left the room. Big Julius shook his head. He sat back and relaxed into the cushions and then stirred his drink with his finger. He took a long sip and sighed. "Ah, that's much better. Now tell me, Mr. Ash, have you ever heard the tale of the Magic Penny?"

"No," replied Ash.

"Are you any good at math?"

"Not really," said Ash. He sipped his tea.

"That's not a problem," said Big Julius, stirring his drink again. "You don't have to be good at math to create a Money Fountain. You only have to be consistent."

Big Julius gazed out of the window while he summoned up the story of the Magic Penny. Then he turned back to Ash.

"Very well. The Magic Penny. Say for instance I were to offer you a choice between taking three million dollars in cash or a single cent that doubles in value every day for thirty days. Which would you choose?"

"The three million of course," said Ash without hesitation.

"Most people would," said Big Julius. "But you've made the wrong choice."

"How so?" Ash frowned. He hated trick questions.

"The cent that doubles in value will lead to greater wealth."

"I don't believe you."

"Okay," said Big Julius taking a deep breath. "You receive the cold hard three million dollars, and your friend goes the Magic Penny route."
"On day five your friend will only have sixteen cents, while you will have three million, which you are free to spend. On day ten your friend will have $5.12. How do you think your friend will be feeling about his choice while he watches you spending your millions?"

"Most probably not happy," conceded Ash.

"After twenty days your friend's penny has grown to $5243. How is he feeling about his choice now?"

"Well," reflected Ash, "I wouldn't be feeling great - so I guess he'd also be a bit miserable.

"Hmm. Hopefully your friend has done the math and is delighted. But let us suppose he hasn't done the math. Jealousy and regret may have raised their heads. You, on the other hand, are enjoying what's left of your three million dollars."

Ash remained alert, though skeptical.

"But then the tide turns in your friend's favor," said Big Julius, his voice becoming intense. "Just a little at first, but the penny that has been doubling in value every day now begins to grow very quickly."

"On day twenty-nine, when you've got what's left of your three million dollars, your friend's cent has grown to be worth 2.7 million. So you now begin to doubt the wisdom of your decision."

"On day thirty the new value of your friend's cent has doubled. It's now 5.3 million dollars. On day thirty-one it turns into 10.5 million dollars. And on day thirty-two - well, I leave the math to you. This is the invisible magic of the compounding effect."

"Eventually your friend's penny turns into a river of money, and then the river becomes a torrent."

Ash sat in disbelief. Could this be the source of the Money Fountain? He warmed to Big Julius. His enthusiasm rose.

"This," said Big Julius, "is how you make money work for you, and not you for it. Allowing interest to compound is the Money Fountain's engine."

"It's incredible," said Ash.

"Oh," chuckled Big Julius, "it's much more than that! It's the Eighth Wonder of the World. And if you keep investing your 10%, with the annual increase for inflation, and reinvest your dividend - your wealth grows faster and faster."

Ash sat dead still. He'd just been handed the keys to his freedom, his liberation from slavery. He needed a moment to compose himself.

"Few things are as impressive as the magic of compound interest," continued Big Julius. "You generate earnings from previous earnings. This is how to make money work for you - and not you for it."

"I'm not sure I understand you completely," said Ash gazing out of the window. But in his mind he saw a Money Fountain - his own Money Fountain.

"The best way to make your money to grow," said Big Julius taking a sip of his drink, "is to invest in something that has a reasonable growth rate linked to the compounding factor - like a share on the stock market. Some place where your investment grows - and you earn dividends at the same time."

Ash was ready to explode with excitement, but he waited for the old man to continue.

"The magic comes when you reinvest your dividend. That's how you generate earnings from previous earnings."

Ash still didn't fully understand, and Big Julius noticed.

"If, for example, you invested $100 in a company and earned a 20% return, at the end of the first year you would have $120. At the end of the next year you would earn 20% on $120. The following year you would earn 20% on $144, and so on. Year after year - your money grows faster."

"In this manner the compounding effect opens a cash stream that multiplies exponentially. At first the flow will be a trickle, but every month the trickle will grow until it becomes a torrent. The trick is to get started."

Ash nodded. That made sense.

"This is why saving 10% of your take-home pay is the key. You have to start now."

Ash was hooked, but he was still unsure how the compounding effect worked. Once again Big Julius noticed.

"Come, let me show you," said Big Julius. He picked up his walking stick and led Ash out the door and up the hill.

Below them was the cattle enclosure.

"Take these cows for example," said Big Julius. He pointed to his herd of cattle.

Ash looked at the herd. He scratched his head.

"In the first year, Mr. Ash, a cow produces one calf. In the second year, you will have two cows that will produce two calves. In the third year, you will have four cows that should produce four calves. If all goes well and you manage to protect your herd and they produce females, in the fourth year you should have eight cows that produce eight calves. By the sixth year, you should have thirty-two cows that produce thirty-two calves. The growth curve is exponential."

"Ah," said Ash slowly as he studied the cows in the compound.

"This is the reason why the old African economy was based on cattle. Even if the female is not pregnant, she still has the potential to produce. This is the compounding principle. But cows also produce males, there is drought, and cattle get sick and die."

Ash thought about cows.

"Unfortunately money invested doesn't double in value in the same way as a Magic Penny," said Big Julius. "Neither does it reproduce like cows in the field. You can however increase the rate your money grows if you reduce the risk and costs. In so doing you can maximize your investment's growth potential."
"Therefore, in order to optimize your income, you need to find a facility that grows at a strong, constant, secure rate."

Then he turned to Ash and grinned: "I think you get the idea?"

"I do," said Ash enthusiastically. He finally got the point.

"The principle of the Magic Penny is the driving force behind the Money Fountain. Once you've set up your Money Fountain you can work out how quickly your money will grow by applying Rule 72."

"Rule 72?" asked Ash.

"Rule 72 gives you an indication as to how long it will take for your money to double."

Ash didn't get it.

"Assuming that your money grows at 15% a year, divide 15 into 72 and you get 4.8 years. That's how long it will take your money to double."

Ash scratched his head again.

"All right," said Big Julius. "Let's take another example Say your money earns 12% interest per year. You divide 12 into 72 and you get six years. If you can find a facility that offers you 30% then your cash doubles in "a little over two years."

"But what about my 10% PYF? Where does that fit in here?"

"That is the source of your Money Fountain – after that, the Magic Penny speeds up the flow."

"Okay. Got it. But then what should I invest my money in?"

"That's a subject for Mrs. Blumkin," replied Big Julius. "That's her strong suit. You've still got much to learn, young man, so take your time and let the information sink in. I will inform TK about the gaps in your knowledge."

They walked down to the homestead and Big Julius held on to Ash's arm to steady himself.

"Having created my own Money Fountain," he said, confiding in Ash, "I'm now enjoying a secure retirement - I'm living off the fruits of my Money Fountain, which is still growing. As you can see, we are comfortable. We are enjoying the finer things in life."

"And the huts down below?" asked Ash.

"My wives live in the compound," said Big Julius.

"You have wives?"

"In traditional custom I have three wives. Under European law, though, I have three girlfriends." The old man grinned.

"Is Molly …?"

"No. She just works here."

"Ah."

"Say, old chap," said Big Julius changing the topic. "Do you have a car?"

Ash answered honestly: "Yes and no."

"I don't understand," said Big Julius frowning.

"I own a car, but I don't have it here. I came by bus. Why?"

"Oh!" said Big Julius with surprise. "You could have driven up here. How are you going to get home?"

"Vuyo said that you'd see to it."

"Ah. In that case would you like to stay for dinner?"

"Thank you. But I've got to get back to my hotel in time to catch my bus. I don't know how I'll do it."

"Don't worry old chap. Molly will run you down after dinner."

Journal entry.

The Magic Penny revealed: my Money Fountain begins to take shape. Shoo, who would have thought that money could be set to work for the individual, not the individual working for money – so easy! Sounds incredible.

My 10% PYF is the source of my Money Fountain – the Magic Penny is the rocket fuel.

Now to invest my 10% in a facility that compounds, but where do I find one?

One secret to go… and what about Conscious Wealth?

Chapter 8. Ray Abrahams

TK soon received word of the deficits Big Julius had detected in Ash's knowledge.
As there was no sense in Ash meeting Mrs. Blumkin before he understood how a stock exchange works, TK had to rectify the situation. A new tutor, Ray Abrahams, was appointed to the task.

The meeting was set to take place at the Olympia Bakery in Kalk Bay. TK hoped that this venue would put an end to Ash's complaints about poor coffee.

From the outset it was obvious to Ash that Ray Abrahams was different. He was young, good looking, and had a flair for the alternative.

Ray was dressed in a charcoal suit with a thin charcoal tie and a crisp white shirt. His black hair was smartly slicked back and he sported a diamond earring in his left ear. He was relaxed and charming, with more than a hint of dash. His smile fizzed with humor and his eyes glinted with a zest for life. Ash was also soon to discover that Ray Abrahams didn't beat about the bush.

"TK tells me that you think Wall Street is the Temple of Greed," said Ray in his opening salvo.

"I've heard it called that," admitted Ash cautiously.

"Do you know what a stock market is? And how it works?"

"Not really. No."

"That's what TK said," replied Ray. He flashed his dazzling smile. "How's your coffee?"

"It's great," said Ash above the din of the busy coffee shop. Indeed, the Olympia's coffee was very good and the foam supported the weight of a sachet of sugar. The milk must be under 145°F, thought Ash. Then he took a sip of his cappuccino. It was warm, silky, sweet, and slightly bitter, with a hint of chocolate and a dusting of cinnamon.

"Have you tried their almond croissants?"

"No, I haven't," replied Ash. "Should I?"

"You've just gotta! The Olympia makes the best almond croissants in the world."

"You're different, Mr Abrahams."

"Different? How?"

"We usually go to places that make terrible coffee."

Ray laughed. He liked being flattered. "There's a time and a place for everything," he said with an offhand smile. Then he beckoned to the waitress, who came over promptly.

"I'd like an almond croissant for my friend," he announced, turning on the charm. Then he turned it off like a switch. He looked at Ash and came straight to the point. "Do you know how a stock exchange works and what a stockbroker does?"

Ash honestly did not know. He looked forward to being tutored. The waitress returned and placed before him a large almond croissant with a dollop of white icing sugar, sprinkled with roasted almonds and a dusting of more icing sugar. It looked fabulous.

"Let's start at the very beginning," said Ray. "Imagine you want to open a coffee shop, but you don't have enough money to do so. Where would you find the money?"

"The bank?"

"Maybe," said Ray. "But if you don't have any assets to use as collateral the bank won't lend you the cash. So you'll have to find the money elsewhere, won't you? But where then?"

Ash shrugged. This was unfamiliar territory.

"You could approach family members and friends or place an ad in the newspaper or online."
"Let's imagine that you're lucky and you find a few people who are prepared to lend you the cash. These people are called investors. Okay?"

"Okay," said Ash nodding.

"When they lend you money," continued Ray, "they've got an interest in your business. They want it to succeed for their own good. They want to be paid back one way or another. It could be understood that they'll get rewarded by taking a share of your business profits."

"Yes," conceded Ash.

"In which case," said Ray, "you'll pay the investors a proportional share of your profit. This is called a dividend."

Ash nodded.

"Now," said Ray, "listen carefully. The only reason people are willing to buy shares in your business is because they want to earn money without having to do the work themselves." Ray grinned to himself. "And in order to do that, they need to have enough money to buy in. The money that investors lend you is called their 'principal'."

Ash nodded again.

"But after a year has passed some of your investors want to get out and move on. They want their principal back to use for other stuff. In other words they want to sell their shares. Where would they find buyers? And where would you find new investors?"

Ash shrugged his shoulders. He was used to earning a salary and saving, not finding investors.

"Now – when big business wants to raise money for a new project it faces the same problem that the aspirant coffee shop owner does. Where do you go to find the start-up cash? Where do you turn? You all face the same problems."

"Tell me," said Ash.

"People who want to raise the capital to start a venture need to raise money from people who have money, just as people who have money to invest need to find companies that pay a dividend."

Ash nodded in agreement.

"Are you with me? Right! When they need to raise money they go to the Stock Exchange."

Ash nodded.
"The stock exchange is a place where people who want to buy and sell shares get together," said Ray sealing his point with a slurp of coffee. "It's a legal market where the money you loan to a business is passed to the business. In return, investors get a share certificate."

"Ah," said Ash - pleased to hear he got a certificate. Legal proof had become a very important issue with him.

"A stock exchange is like a supermarket," continued Ray, "which sells a wide variety of products - many of which are similar and compete against each other. Now – the main reason people go to a supermarket is because it's convenient. They can do all their shopping in one place. A stock exchange is a supermarket for shares. Do you understand?"

"You mean investors with an amount of principal go to the stock exchange to purchase shares?"

"Good man!" said Ray flashing his brilliant smile. "Say - aren't you going to try your croissant?"

"Yes. Yes. I was listening to you."

"Well, let's eat and talk at the same time."

Ash nodded.

"Here," said Ray, "let me show you how to eat an almond croissant." Stretching across the table, Ray broke off a piece of Ash's croissant, dunked it in his own coffee and popped it into his mouth. Then he savored the flavor. "The best part is licking your fingers afterwards," said Ray. He licked his fingers with gusto.

Ash broke off a piece of his croissant, dunked it and popped it into his mouth. Ray was right - the combination of flavors was perfect. He was finding the lesson both informative and enjoyable.

"So," said Ray, licking his fingers again. "When a company wants to raise money on the stock exchange it approaches the stock exchange and requests to be listed. Once the company has met the legal requirements set down by the stock exchange, it becomes a listed company. And when a company becomes listed it can legally sell shares in itself, to the public. And it'll usually issue many millions of shares."

Ash began to get it - the secret of how money could be set to work for him, and not he for it, was slowly being revealed.

"When the stock exchange is open, stock brokers buy or sell shares at the current market price – for their clients."
"That job used to be done by the guys shouting on the floor of the stock exchange, but they've been replaced by electronic trading platforms."

"What's that?" asked Ash, licking his fingers,

"Stockbrokers now enter transactions directly - via trading platforms over the internet." Ray smiled to himself.

"Ah. Right." Ash popped another piece of croissant into his mouth, again savoring the sweet almond-and-coffee flavor. "Then how do I buy shares?"

"About that, it's best for you to wait until you see Mrs. Blumkin. She'll talk to you about how to buy. My job is to tutor you in the rudimentary functioning of the third aspect, which is how to make money work for you."

Ray took another piece of Ash's croissant, dunked it, popped it into his mouth, and licked his fingers.

"The secret to the Money Fountain remains the same," he continued. "PYF 10%, invest in an instrument that compounds, and reinvest the dividend."

He looked at Ash to see if he was following. Once satisfied he continued: "When a company wishes to raise money on the stock exchange, it goes through the legal process of getting listed. Got me? Once the company is listed, it becomes a publicly listed company and it's then able to sell shares in itself."

Ash nodded.

"When you buy shares in a company, and get a share certificate, you are entitled to attend the company's Annual General Meeting, vote members onto the board, and receive a dividend if the company declares one."

"I don't understand how the price of a share is established."

The question impressed Ray. Sadly there was no simple explanation for Ash but Ray tried: "The initial pricing of a share is a complex process, but each share is given a price when it's first listed. The future value of that share depends on how well the company is doing and how many investors want to buy shares in it. This is called the share's 'market price.'"

Ash nodded.

"When a company makes a profit, that profit is divided by the number of shares it's sold, and each shareholder gets paid a dividend – if the company declares one. The dividend is the money you receive when you let your savings work for you. Right?"

"Understood."

"If the company does not make a profit, then you won't get a dividend and the value of your shares could drop."

Ash swallowed.

"But when a company does well, and more investors want to own shares in it, its share price goes up. This is known as capital growth."

"If a company is doing badly, people are often inclined to sell their shares. When there are more sellers than buyers, the market price of a share drops. This is a bad time to sell, but sometimes a good time to buy."

A bus drove past and its shadow briefly darkened the restaurant though the hubbub indoors didn't dim.

"The good news is that when a company loses money, you are not responsible for its losses. Your losses are limited to the price and the number of shares you own. It's not like a Ponzi scheme where you lose all your money."

"Why did you say 'when a company loses money'?" Ash frowned.

"When?" asked Ray. "I'll be frank, Mr Ash. All companies go through bad patches. It's not if - it's when. Right?"

"Right," said Ash.

"Some investors buy and sell shares quickly - buying when shares are cheap and selling when the price rises. These investors are called 'speculators'. This might sound like a good idea, but there are many reasons why it isn't."

"Why?" asked Ash. "It makes sense to me."

"Speculating is like gambling – it's risky and stressful. You have to know the companies extremely well in order to choose the best shares to buy. And brokers charge fees and commissions – which are deducted from your profits. So the more you speculate the more your costs go up. Now one of the main aims of successful investing is to reduce your costs. Once again, this is a job for Mrs. Blumkin."

Ash looked forward to meeting her.

"Speculators cause the share prices to rise and fall over a short period," continued Ray. "This is known as volatility and this scenario might not be in the investor's best interest. You with me?"

"Yes." Ash nodded again. Ray was tempted to start calling Ash 'Noddy' but he realized that Ash was a beginner and very nervous, so he overcame the impulse. Instead, he grinned.

"Can a listed company issue new shares?" asked Ash.

"Yes. A listed company may issue new shares. This is referred to as a 'rights issue'."

"Are all companies listed on the stock exchange?"

"No," said Ray. "A company that is not listed on the stock exchange is referred to as an 'unlisted company'. Unlisted companies also sell shares in themselves, but their shares are not protected or governed by the rules of the stock exchange."

"Would my coffee shop – let's pretend, for example - be an unlisted company?" asked Ash.

"Yes," said Ray. "That kind of investment might best be referred to as venture capital or private equity."

"When is it best to sell one's shares?" asked Ash. He was getting ahead of himself, thought Ray. One step at a time....

"That's also a job for Mrs. Blumkin," he replied. "But the basic principle is to sell shares when the price is high, and buy when they're low. I mean - of course you can sell your shares whenever you want, but would that be wise? Selling negates the principle of the Magic Penny, so why would you want to do that?"

To Ray's relief, Ash sat back and calmed down.

"And this brings me back to my original question. What is a stockbroker? Do you know?"

"I don't," replied Ash honestly.

"A stockbroker is a member of the stock exchange and is licensed to trade shares on behalf of clients. He or she is your link to the stock market. Part of the service offered by a stockbroker is to advise a client on which shares to buy, sell or hold."

Ash nodded.

"But be warned," said Ray ominously.

"Stock brokers have fees, commissions, and conditions. This is how they make their money. These fees vary from broker to broker and, if you aren't careful, these costs will affect your profit. So choose wisely. The key issue remains the same - reduce the commission charged by the middleman and invest the savings. Mrs. Blumkin will advise you."

Ash was beginning to grasp the greater mysteries of how money could be set to work for him.

"We promote a long-term stress-free investment strategy," said Ray taking a sip of coffee. "But the decision to sell your shares will always remain yours."

Then, taking a long look at 'Nodder' Ash, Ray summed up the lesson: "You now know what a stock market is, what a broker is, and how to buy a share. You also know that each trade you make has a cost, and the more trades you make the more your costs rise. The aim of successful investing is to limit those costs – and then invest the difference in your Money Fountain."

"Yes."

"Finally," said Ray with a big smile, "I think you're ready for Mrs. Blumkin. I shall inform TK. How about a drink and something to eat?"

"Sounds great," said Ash.

"Your shout."

"My shout?" asked Ash. "I don't understand."

"Oh," said Ray innocently. "I don't have any cash on me right now. You don't mind picking up the tab, do you?"

"No, no," stammered Ash. "Not at all."

Journal entry.

Ray. What a character. Coffee was great. Lunch was excellent. Stock market revealed. Didn't realize I knew so little. Seek investment that offers compounding facility — The Magic Penny.

Ray's list of Investment Do's and Don'ts
- *Invest 10% of take-home pay... can do.*
- *Never go into debt in order to invest (good idea).*
- *Invest for the long term (fair).*
- *Reinvest your dividend (understood).*
- *Invest in quality (too poor to risk buying second-hand stuff).*

•Buy shares that will grow.
•Stick to the basics (right).
•Do not put all your eggs in one basket.
•Check all the charges and make sure I understand them before I commit.
•Be cautious of sages (yikes!).
•Don't let your investments rule your life (big ask, but will try).

To bed now. God bless TK and the Fellowship, without whom I would not be.

Chapter 9. Mrs. Rose Blumkin

Mrs. Blumkin lived in a large colonial mansion that held a prime position at the Muizenberg end of Sunrise Beach. From there the beach curled far around False Bay until it reached the Hottentots Holland Mountains on the other side, where the sun rose.

Ash had reason to feel good. He had climbed to the pinnacle of financial success, lost it all, crawled through the dark valley of depression and survived. And now he found himself close to the bright peaks of a new summit.

A fresh breeze rustled the palm fronds as he skipped up the steps to the front door. Next to the door was a fountain in which the water tinkled merrily. From the pool a lotus flower looked up at him with its sky-blue eye. Ash could have sworn that it winked.

He rang the front doorbell and turned to admire the view. As he did so a dashing young woman bounded up the steps.

Ash introduced himself and explained why he was there.

"Oh! Hello. I'm Juliet, Mrs. Blumkin's assistant. I'm very pleased to meet you at last. I've heard so much about you."

"Thank you," said Ash blushing. "Is Mrs. Blumkin in?"

"She is indeed. Please come inside."

Juliet opened the front door and invited Ash into the opulent lobby. This opened into a large dining room which in turn led out through double doors, and onto a patio with yet another fountain. Ash would have been happy to linger in this room, but Juliet led him briskly down a long corridor.

At the end they came to a door and Juliet knocked softly. There was no answer. She opened the door and invited Ash through. He found himself in a large study with bay windows that overlooked the sea. There was a generous fireplace. In front of this, and taking up the center of the room, were two dark leather couches on either side of a broad coffee table. In one of the window bays, facing the glorious view, stood a beautifully polished desk. Its gleaming surface was clear, apart from a desk lamp, a laptop and a phone.

"Please take a seat," said Juliet. "Mrs. Blumkin will join you presently." Ash liked the dimples in her smile. He sat down on a leather couch.

From the couch Ash looked around - admiring the wood-paneled room. Like a library, it had extensive shelves filled with well-thumbed books. A large chandelier hung from the ornate gold-painted pressed-steel ceiling.

Above the fireplace, in prime position in the room, was an oil painting. It was striking. It showed a stern woman with a blue-tinted face, bright red lips and a thick crop of black hair. She wore a beautiful ornate top rendered in gold, which shimmered in the light. Ash liked the top, but the background was so rough that Ash thought it unfinished. He was fascinated by the woman's distant, removed pose. It was at once haughty and tranquil. He liked the painting. He liked its strong energy. He had no idea that it was the famous Blue Lady – painted by Vladimir Tretchikoff from a model who's name was Miss Wong. It was a highly acclaimed, sought-after canvas. There was an audio backdrop which Ash found exquisite. He didn't know, but it was the Adagio from Mozart's Violin Concerto No 3. He still needed much refining, but that task lay in the future.

Ash didn't hear Mrs. Blumkin enter. He was still absorbed in his admiration of the grandeur of the room.

She walked briskly across. "You must be Ash," she said - extending her hand.

It was immediately obvious to Ash why the other members of the Fellowship referred to Mrs. Blumkin with such deference. She was a no-nonsense person. She was short and stocky and she stood solidly on her two feet which were clad in dark shoes with wide non-slip heels. She was old-school, from an age when women still 'did' their hair, and Mrs. Blumkin had done hers with a perm and mauve rinse, which matched her mauve slack-suit. She wore a double-string pearl necklace and earrings to match. Ash strongly suspected that he was finally in the presence of the oracle. And indeed he was.

"Yes," said Ash. He stood up promptly and took her hand. "Thank you for seeing me."

"The pleasure's all mine," said Mrs. Blumkin, taking the seat opposite Ash. When she was comfortable she fixed Ash with a bright no-nonsense look.

"TK tells me that you're ready to learn the third secret of the Money Fountain."

"I hope so," ventured Ash nervously.

"Would you like something to drink?"

"Thank you. That would be nice."

"What's your poison?" The old lady had a merry glint in her eye.

"I don't drink alcohol," confessed Ash. "Tea would be nice. Or just water."

Mrs. Blumkin pushed a buzzer.

"Juliet?"

"Yes ma'am."

"Juliet, please bring Mr Ash a cup of tea."

"And for you, ma'am?"

"I'll have my sherry now, thank you."

"Isn't it a bit early?" Juliet's voice was clear on the intercom, and in his mind Ash again saw the mischievous dimples.

"Thank you, Juliet. That will do. Now will be fine."

"Warren Buffet," began Mrs. Blumkin, turning to face Ash. "When Warren Buffet was a boy, he earned his pocket money by delivering newspapers, collecting bottles and selling second-hand golf balls – which he paid a friend to retrieve from an icy pond."

"In 1942, when he was twelve, he had saved up a hundred and twenty dollars. In those days that was a large sum of money, and he used his savings to buy shares in a company called Cities Services Preferred. He bought three shares for himself and, using her money, three for his sister Doris. The total cost to Warren, for his three shares, was $114.75, meaning that each share cost $38.25.

"As luck would have it," said Mrs. Blumkin, "the share price tanked, and within a short while the value of the shares dropped to $27. And every day, on their way to school, much to Warren's embarrassment, Doris reminded him that the value of her stock was falling.

"When the share price recovered to $40 Warren sold, netting them each a small $5.25 profit. As if to prove a point, the price of Cities Services Preferred then soared to $202 a share. In his rush to claim a quick profit Warren had lost out on a potential profit of $490. That's a substantially bigger profit, isn't it?" Mrs. Blumkin looked hard at Ash and cleared her throat.

"From this experience," she continued, "Warren Buffet learned three lessons that he never forgot: don't overly fixate on the price paid for a share, don't rush in and grab a small profit, and don't invest other people's money."
"Warren internalized these lessons and went on to become one of the richest men in the world."

Ash nodded. He got the message.

"Now let's get to the point, Mr. Ash. What is the ideal investment?"

"I've been trying to figure that out myself," said Ash politely, scratching his head.

"The perfect investment," said Mrs. Blumkin, "is one where your money does all the work - and you do none." Then she smoothed her slacks, folded her arms and continued. "This is what we mean when we say 'create a Money Fountain that will flow endlessly towards you'. That is what it's all about."

"It sounds perfect."

"Indeed it is," confirmed Mrs. Blumkin briskly. "But you can only achieve that when you get the basics of the operating systems in place."
She ticked them off on her fingers. "Know the difference between essential and non-essential spending; get a job; save 10% PYF; 20% for debtors; own a modest house; write a will; take out life insurance." Ash noticed the rings on her fingers.

"Yes," said Ash. 'I understand that clearly."

"And you now understand how the Magic Penny works?"

"Yes."

"And how the stock market works?"

"The basics, yes," replied Ash.

"This is good," said Mrs. Blumkin. "And now you are ready to start investing?"

"Yes!" said Ash.

"Wonderful. Once again the team has done an excellent job."

The door at the far end of the study opened and Juliet entered, carrying a silver tray.

"Ah, Juliet. Juliet, have you met Mr Ash?"

"Yes, we met on the steps, thank you," said Juliet as she placed the drinks on the table. Then she retreated and closed the door.

"Right," said Mrs. Blumkin rubbing her hands together. "Let's get down to business." She picked up her drink and examined it. Then she took a careful sip of sherry. "Mr. Ash, you are now ready to learn the third and final secret of the Money Fountain."

Ash held his teacup on his knee as Mrs. Blumkin continued briskly.

"The shares you seek are those that grow by an average of 15% or more a year, pay regular dividends, have locked-in fees, have no hidden costs, are legal, and offer you the choice to reinvest your dividend."

"Like the compounding effect of the Magic Penny?" asked Ash.

"Exactly!" Mrs. Blumkin smiled. "We also promote a long-term investment strategy of twenty-five-plus years.

"Why is that?

"Because the longer you leave your money in your Money Fountain the faster it grows."

"Is that a certainty?" enquired Ash.

"Virtually," said Mrs. Blumkin. Then she continued. "So you've worked hard for your money, saved your 10%, and you're now ready to start investing?"

"Yes," responded Ash with enthusiasm. "I am!"

"Do you understand risk?"

"No," he said.

Mrs. Blumkin murmured 'risk' softly to herself while she studied the ceiling. When she located the correct file in the cabinet of her thoughts she raised her glass, said "cheers" and took a sip. She didn't put the glass down, but cradled it thoughtfully in her fingers.

"The dictionary," she continued, "defines risk as 'the chance of something going wrong'. For the sake of convenience I shall try to explain risk as simply as possible."

"Thank you," said Ash. He was a devotee of simple.

"Compare the risk of investing to the risk of crossing a busy street. Can you see an image of a busy street with a lot of traffic in your mind, Mr Ash?"

Ash nodded. He liked images. He found them easy to understand.

"When you cross a street, there is always a risk that you might get run over, so it's best to consider the different ways in which you can get across."

Ash nodded. Crossing the street was clear enough.

"Where you cross will depend on how fit and alert you are. If you are cautious or old and use a walking frame, then it's best to choose the safest options. If you are young and full of energy," said Mrs. Blumkin, taking a larger sip of her sherry, "you might try a high-risk crossing – like running across between the traffic. As you well know - there's a good chance you will get run over. And if you do get run over it will be your fault - and you will have to suffer the consequences."

"Fair's fair," said Ash nodding.

"Consider then," said Mrs. Blumkin, "that the flow of money through the economy is the busy street that you're about to cross. And now you have to choose the best place to do so."

Ash nodded.

"The first thing you have been taught about crossing a street is to look left and right to see if there is any approaching traffic. This is like assessing your entry point into the stock market. Do you go through a broker or do you use an online platform?"

She took a small sip of her sherry and continued.

"Once you've resolved this, the next hurdle you come to is what shares to buy. There are various options. The point at which you cross the street can be seen as selecting the kinds of shares you want to buy. There are various options - conservative, medium-risk, high-risk, and just plain silly.

"As you have been taught, the best place to cross a street is at a pedestrian crossing or a regulated traffic intersection – when the traffic's has come to a stop. Are you still with me?"

"Yes."

Mrs. Blumkin finished her sherry. Then she leaned across and pressed the buzzer.

"Yes, ma'am?"

"Juliet, I am so sorry - I've knocked over my sherry. Please bring me another."

"Yes, ma'am."

"Right, where were we?" Mrs. Blumkin pursed her lips. "Yes. That's right. Pressing the pedestrian crossing button and bringing all the traffic to a stop. It's safe, and if you do get run over you'll be covered by insurance. This is like leaving your money in a savings account in a bank. This is a safe option but you will most probably lose money."

"Why?

"Because the bank will pay you a modest interest - and if the inflation rate exceeds the interest rate then your money will shrink."

"Ah! As bad as that?"

"Yes," nodded Mrs. Blumkin. "Or you can cross the road when the traffic is turning while the green pedestrian light is flashing. If you're fit and alert, then this is a relatively safe option. This could be considered to be an ETF."

"ETF? What's that?" asked Ash. "Isn't an ETF what happens when you make payments with online banking?"

"No, Mr. Ash! Those are EFT's - electronic fund transfers. An ETF is an Exchange-Traded Fund." Mrs. Blumkin looked hard at him. "But please be patient and I'll come back to that."

Juliet appeared with the sherry decanter, recharged Mrs. Blumkin's glass, and was just about to depart when Mrs. Blumkin interrupted her.

"Thank you Juliet," said Mrs. Blumkin. "You may leave the decanter on the table."

"But …?"

"Thank you, Juliet. That will be all."

Juliet put the decanter down, hesitated, and then retreated. Taking up her glass, Mrs. Blumkin continued. "Now – back to crossing the street, Mr. Ash. You can, of course, always try to sneak across against the light - when the pedestrian light is red for you and green for oncoming traffic."

Ash narrowed his eyes. He thought about it.

"This, of course, is only safe if you are fit and alert and you can cross the street quickly. You can compare this to speculators - who cause the market's volatility. This is stressful and if you get run over, as I said before, it will be your fault." Mrs. Blumkin looked hard at Ash again.

"Alternatively, you can jaywalk and cross the road at any point. This is dangerous and could be considered to be like venture capital. Venture capital is when you invest in a new company but get do not get the security of listed company. There is a high degree of risk - but those who invested in Apple shares will tell you it was worth the risk."

"The highest risk of all," continued Mrs. Blumkin, "is to try to cross a road at night when you are drunk, wearing dark clothing, in a place where there are no street lights. You would agree that this is stupid, and one should expect to meet with disaster in that situation. Crossing the street under those conditions might be compared to a high-risk investment that offers returns that are too good to be true - like a pyramid scheme or a Ponzi scheme. But believe you me, Mr. Ash, many big fish have found themselves caught by this baited hook."

Ash recognized his own folly and he laughed nervously.

"These schemes promise fabulous returns, but they are illegal. Only those who get out early don't get burnt. If you want to throw your money away, then go for this option. I believe that you've had direct experience of a Ponzi scheme?" Mrs. Blumkin shot him a glance and stole a sip of sherry.

"Yes," admitted Ash. "That, and emeralds from Thailand."

"I see," said Mrs. Blumkin, tapping her finger against her glass.

"So," she continued, "let's assess your best options. You might agree that crossing the street when the traffic-flow is turning and the green pedestrian light flashing is the best option. There is a small risk, but it's generally safe. If something goes wrong, you have protection."

Ash agreed.

"Very well. Now before I explain the best investment option to you, let's first examine the performance of stock markets. On average, the stock market doubles in value every four and a half years."

Ash's eyes widened. That was interesting to know.

"So if you invested $1000 in the stock market and left it there for twenty-five years, it would be worth $20 000. But if you invested $1000 a month and adjust this payment annually to match inflation and, let's say, the average annual return on the investment is 15% per year, after 25 years it would be worth $5 625 622, before costs."

Ash felt excitement rising inside himself. He had a vague understanding of the Magic Penny, but this growth astounded him. He sat up.

"So if you invested $1000 per month over the entire 25-year period you will only have invested $300 000 odd while your investment will have grown by roughly five million dollars. This fabulous growth was achieved because you invested in an instrument that compounded your dividend, and you increased your 10% PYF by inflation every year. That is all it took."

"So even if you can only afford to invest a few hundred dollars a month - you'll still win. The reason for this is because the stock market is the ultimate arbiter."

"The ultimate arbiter?" asked Ash. It seemed to him that this position was reserved for God. He was awed.

"Everybody has an inbuilt fear of a stock market crash. Just as people fear a wildfire, they fear a stock market crash. This fear is based on the market crash of 1929. But when you apply logic, the 1929 stock market crash is not quite the train smash everybody makes it out to be."

"I don't understand."

"If for instance" said Mrs. Blumkin pausing for another sip, "in 1928, the year before the Wall Street Crash, you had $10 000 invested in an index, ten years later your investment would have been worth $7000. You would only have lost $3000 - not quite the catastrophe everybody made it out to be."

Ash pondered this.

"Consider this then," continued Mrs. Blumkin. "If you'd invested $100 a month over the same period and compounded your dividend, then your money would have grown to $15 000."

Ash took a sip of his tea.

"Even though you would have invested $12 000 over the period, you would have endured the greatest stock market collapse of all time and still emerged with a $3000 profit."

Ash wasn't entirely impressed.

"The point I am making," said Mrs. Blumkin, "is that in the long-term markets recover and grow. They have survived world wars, dot.com busts, housing bubbles, and credit crunch implosions. The stock market beats inflation, bank interest rates, government bonds, mutual funds – and it doubles in value every four-an-half years."

Ash was even more impressed.

"The operating principle to making money on the stock exchange," continued Mrs. Blumkin, "is to own as much of it as possible for as long as possible."

"How do I do that?"

"Success can be explained by five factors," said Mrs. Blumkin. "Time, 10% PYF, invested in an instrument that compounds, reinvesting your dividends and increasing your 10% by inflation each year."

"That sounds simple," said Ash nodding.

"It's important to remember," said Mrs. Blumkin, "making money on the stock market is not about being clever and trying to outperform the market. If you try this you'll never stop running, and as you well know, one gets exhausted. Even worse, in the end worrying about the market will count against you. Also, don't put your faith in investment advisors or gurus."

"Oh? Why not?"

"Remember - brokers, advisors and gurus make their money from fees and commissions, not from investments. These costs cause 'drag' which erodes the performance of your portfolio."
"Basically, they are drinking from your Money Fountain while building their own."

Mrs. Blumkin nestled back into her chair and continued. "As I will explain shortly, growing your wealth on the stock market is actually simple. The operating principle is to own shares in the biggest companies for as long as possible. And even when the market fluctuates, stay the course. Remember - success is about how much of the market you own - and how long you own it for."

Ash nodded.

"And never speculate on the market," said Mrs. Blumkin. "That's gambling. Occasionally you might win, but in the long run you will lose."

"I understand," said Ash, erasing such fantasies from his mind.

"Another point," said Mrs. Blumkin, "is that investors who constantly track the market and listen to the financial news actually make half the money of those who pay no attention to it at all."

"You can't be serious?"

"But I am," said Mrs. Blumkin. "We, of the Fellowship, have a simple strategy that works exactly as a fountain should."

"I like the sound of this," said Ash - his excitement rising.

"Now let's examine the different investment options – and see which one best fits the street-crossing solution."

"Unit trusts, also known as mutual funds," continued Mrs. Blumkin, "are not a great investment option - because their managers spend most of their time trying to outperform the market, but the vast majority end up doing worse. Over a ten-year period, those that survived lag behind the market by 80%."

"Why is that?" asked Ash.

"Because, once again, their costs, fees, and commissions work against them," said Mrs. Blumkin taking a sip of cherry before continuing. "The key principle to investing is 'don't be greedy.' And after that, successful investing relies on limiting costs."

"How do I do that?"

"All investments have costs related to buying and selling shares, and there are also fees for receiving advice. The aim is to reduce your fees."

Ash nodded.

"The rules of wealth creation are straightforward and simple," said Mrs. Blumkin putting down her glass. Then she ticked off the points once again on her fingers. "Wealth multiplies happily for those who invest wisely, it needs and clings to protection, it abandons those who invest in businesses they know little about, it flees from those who aren't skilled in working with it. It shuns those who try to extract impossible returns from it - and those with little or no experience in dealing with investments. It also shuns those who gamble. Without wisdom, wealth is easily lost."

Ash recognized many of these lessons from his own personal experience.

"When it comes to investments, the old adage applies: 'if it sounds too good to be true, it probably is'. Avoid pyramid schemes. Don't invest in businesses you know nothing about, and don't invest in a project where you will end up having to do the work yourself."

"But with wisdom," said Mrs Blumkin emphatically, "those who do not have wealth can easily acquire it. So let logic prevail - work with the market, go with its flow."

"But what should I invest in?"

The door opened and Juliet entered carrying a silver tray with two clean glasses and a bottle of mineral water.

"Yes, Juliet?" asked Mrs. Blumkin.

"I thought Mr. Ash's tea might be cold so I've brought some water."

"That's great," said Ash before Mrs. Blumkin could intervene. "Thank you."

Juliet filled both glasses, placing one in front of Mrs. Blumkin, giving her a hard look. Unperturbed, Mrs. Blumkin continued.

"The best time, Mr. Ash, to plant an oak tree was twenty years ago. The second best time to plant an oak tree is now."

"What do you mean?"

"If you haven't started investing yet then I recommend that you start investing now. To start, you don't have to invest a lot of money, but if you start now it's so much easier than starting behind the game."

"But what should I invest in?" asked Ash impatiently.

"There are many investment options to choose from," said Mrs. Blumkin. "The trick is to pick the one that fits your ultimate goals in life."

Ash responded: "That means saving 10% of my income and investing it in an instrument that compounds, and reinvesting the dividend."

Mrs. Blumkin clapped her hands. "You've got it, my good student Mr. Ash! That is what Pay-Yourself-First means."

Ash smiled - he did get it.

"Do this by stop order. It will bring a lot of money, joy, and peace into your life. Now, to answer your question - we have sourced an instrument that will not require you to be worried about how your shares are performing.

Ash was filled with anticipation - he had finally arrived at his Land of Dreams.

"You are looking for a vehicle that will offer 15% annual growth, or more, where your principal is secure, will pay a dividend, offers you the ability to reinvest and compound your dividend, and the agreement is legal."

"That sounds perfect," said Ash. The picture was becoming crystal clear.

Mrs. Blumkin studied Ash's face. Yes, she said to herself, he's getting it. She continued:

"Risk is inextricably bound to the length of time you hold an asset. If you can hold an asset for twenty-five years then you can ignore the market's volatility. Ultimately, the needle of the compass always points back to ETFs."

Ash could sense he was close to ground zero.

"So, do you know what an ETF is?" asked Mrs. Blumkin.

"No!"

"Do you know what an index is?"

Ash shook his head. Nope, he had no idea.

"There are many different companies listed on a stock exchange - and many of these companies operate in similar fields. Mining, banking, energy, or retail sectors, for example. For convenience the stock exchange groups these companies according to the sector they operate in, or their size. When these companies are grouped together they form an 'index'."

Ash nodded.

"There are also world indices that include the world's largest companies regardless of where they are based. One such index is the S&P Global 100."

"Indices?" asked Ash.

"That's the plural form of index."

Ash scratched his head. "Could you please explain what an index is again?"

"An index," repeated Mrs. Blumkin with infinite patience, "can be thought of as a basket of shares that includes a number of different companies. Some indices focus on a particular sector of the economy; others group companies according to their size. For example," she continued, "the most famous index is the Dow Jones Industrial Index. It comprises the thirty best-performing companies in the United States. There are other indices such as the FTSE, Nikkei and the JSE Top 40."

The names were vaguely familiar to Ash.

"There are many different indices. Some are industry or sector specific; others focus on the best-performing companies and some focus on companies that are environmentally friendly."

Ash was catching on quickly.

"So, an index is made up of different companies and the weighted average price of all their shares is what we call the index value."

"Wouldn't it be great if I could buy shares in one index instead of buying shares in each company!" exclaimed Ash.

"That's exactly what an ETF is," said Mrs. Blumkin. "It's a listed investment fund traded on a stock exchange. And it trades just like any other listed share. Except that, just as you say, instead of buying one share in each company, when you buy an ETF you are buying a share in all the companies listed in that ETF."

Ash got that.

"An ETF also gives you the opportunity to buy or sell whenever you like, just like any other share traded on the stock exchange. And if a few of these companies do badly, the rest pull the shares price up. Do you understand?"

"So you mean all my eggs won't be in the same basket," said Ash.

"Exactly," said Mrs Blumkin. "Because the share price of an ETF is based on the average price of all the shares in the index – all your eggs are not in the same basket."

"Who owns an ETF?" asked Ash. His interest was growing by leaps and bounds.

"Most ETFs are owned and listed by large financial institutions like banks. They are known as the ETF issuer."

Ash nodded.

"When this basket of shares, or ETF, gets listed on the stock exchange, it trades just like any other share, but it gives you the broadest possible diversification at the smallest possible cost."

Ash was unsure of this point.

"John Bogle," said Mrs Blumkin, "the man who created the first ETF forty years ago, was famous for saying 'forget trying to find the needle in the haystack. Buy the haystack.'"

Ash didn't quite understand this.

"What he meant was why waste your time trying to find the little gems when you can buy the whole market."

Ash got it. Mrs. Blumkin picked up her glass of water.

"How do I buy an ETF?" asked Ash.

"You can buy shares in an ETF by placing an order with your stockbroker, online trading broker, or the ETF issuer," said Mrs. Blumkin. "The beauty of an ETF is that the costs are limited."

Ash looked puzzled.

"When you buy shares in an ETF you are buying one share in all the companies listed in that ETF. So instead of paying brokerage fees and commission on shares in all the companies, you only pay once - but you get a share in all forty companies. And there are no hidden costs or charges because the stock broking firm receives no commission other than the brokerage fees they charge for the ETF trade, and these fees have been negotiated and agreed upon upfront."

"That limits the cost of the middleman," said Ash smugly.

"Good student," said Mrs. Blumkin. "And your savings can be invested in your Money Fountain."

"That makes a lot of sense," grinned Ash. "Are dividends taxed?"

"Yes," replied Mrs. Blumkin. "At 15% a year, and there's also capital gains tax (CGT). But CGT only applies if you sell your shares after three years."

"Why should my shares be taxed twice?" asked Ash. "Surely I can't make a profit then?"

"The citizen's reward," said Mrs. Blumkin, "is a stable country and economy."

Ash conceded the point and resolved to pay his taxes.

"Besides," said Mrs. Blumkin, "only the dividend gets taxed, not your lump-sum investment."

"What security does an ETF offer?" asked Ash.

"My, my," said Mrs. Blumkin. "You have certainly grown."

Ash smiled. "I'm fortunate to have excellent tutors."

"I'll drink to that," said Mrs. Blumkin raising her glass of water. "Cheers."

Ash raised his glass in salute and took a sip.

"ETFs which track an index tick all the right protection boxes," said Mrs. Blumkin.

"They are legal, you can sell or buy an ETF if and when you need to, your principal is returned to you when you sell, dividends are paid four times a year, you can reinvest your dividend, and, because an ETF is diversified, all your eggs, as you pointed out, are in one basket. But - a note of caution. You must only invest in an ETF that tracks an index."

Ash made a mental note of this.

"The list of an ETF's good stuff goes on," said Mrs. Blumkin enthusiastically. "An ETF is required to be fully transparent. This means that the ETF's performance is published every day. An ETF is also a safe place to invest because it is backed 100% by physical security."

"What is physical security?" asked Ash.

"Physical security is the share that you've bought. It's called 'physical' because it can be bought and sold at a price determined by the market."

"Does this mean I get my money back when I sell my shares?" asked Ash.

"Yes."

The penny was dropping. Ash was close to the goal. He now understood how purchasing shares in an ETF made sense. It offered a better return than the bank, and was more secure than anything he had previously heard or learned about. And, over time it offered stupendous growth. He gave a small enthusiastic chuckle.

"Investing in an ETF is like crossing the street at a traffic light when the green pedestrian light is flashing," said Mrs. Blumkin. "It's safe and you don't have to bother about checking on the prices of your stocks - because you know that in the long term the stock market will grow. This frees you up so that you get on with enjoying the finer aspects of your life while your money works for you."

This worked for Ash. He felt thrilled.

"Once you've chosen your investments and settled on a workable routine, sit back and enjoy your youth, your good health, your family, and the incredible planet that you live on - and let your money work for you." Mrs. Blumkin folded her hands and smiled. Then she challenged him:

"So now that you understand how ETFs work, what index would you invest in?"

Ash was unsure. He felt spoilt for choice.

"This is where Conscious Wealth comes to the fore. An index usually lists companies according to their size or sector, but some of these companies might have rapacious labor policies, others have an oversized carbon footprint, or conduct business that is in one or another way harmful to the environment. Would you like to invest in a company with such bad practices?"

"Not really."

"Good. Now remember, without a destination there can't be a journey."

"Yes," said Ash. "That is true."

"Well - the Conscious Wealth ETF has yet to created, but the aim is to invest in the future without cutting corners in pursuit of profit margins. That is our destination. The environment has borne this cost for far too long, and it cannot sustain our narrow-minded profit incentive for much longer. We have to do more, and we can. "

"Conscious Wealth is concerned with the pursuit of a higher purpose. Conscious Wealth states that the way in which we generate profit must change if environment and businesses are going to survive," said Mrs. Blumkin.

"Conscious Wealth seeks to invest in businesses with integrity and high environmental standards that serve all parties - and that list includes workers, suppliers, customers, investors, the community, and the environment."

Ash got the message. He liked this vision.

"Conscious Wealth," continued Mrs. Blumkin, "supports fair trade, where suppliers of certain products have to fulfill certain minimum standards, such as sending their staff's children to school. For this reason, when you buy coffee with the fair trade label, you are paying more for it because the beans purchased have a real cost associated with their growing and harvesting. This doesn't mean that profit is negated. It means that the real price is paid for the product."

"So you mean Conscious Wealth creates wealth that is good for the environment?"

"Yes!" said Mrs. Blumkin. "And what's more - because it's not usury-based there is no bad karma. Like Mahatma Gandhi's policy of passive resistance, conscious wealth paves the way to a sustainable future without conflict. It steers investment capital away from polluting companies to environmentally friendly companies, without the need for confrontation."

She paused here, and looked squarely at Ash.

"Instead of voting with your feet, you will now be voting with your wallet, and we all know that money talks. This is the non-violent change that the world's been seeking."

Ash was staggered by the simplicity of the vision.

"If you stick to the rules," added Mrs. Blumkin, "for twenty-five years and keep on investing your PYF 10%, adjusted annually for inflation, and reinvest your dividend - you will become financially independent. And if you keep to the plan for longer you will be very wealthy indeed. All you need is to be consistent and patient. It's as simple as that."

Mrs. Blumkin paused again, and then added:

"Even though the first few years will be tough, once you've adjusted your lifestyle to 90% of your take home pay, life will become easier. After twenty-five years you will be financially secure, and free."

Journal entry.

Mr.s Blumkin, what a peach. Excellent! ETF… WOW!

Investment profile:
Seek stock that grows by 15% per year or more.
Pays a dividend every three or four months.
No hidden costs.
Can recover your principal.
Offers the opportunity to reinvest dividend (compounding effect).
Invest for twenty-five-plus years.
Own as much of the stock exchange as you can for as long as possible.

Free at last!

Chapter 10. Pay It Forward

Ash entered the Cape Town International Airport terminal building early because he liked being early. He found that when he got going early all the traffic lights were green for him - and when he got going late they all seemed to be red.

Time had flown, as it does when one is having fun. The dark years had passed and he was once again enjoying days of abundance. Ash had left the hardware store and he was now promoting Money Fountain Investments. Grey hair had appeared on his temples. This wasn't due to anxiety. It was due to the passing of time. It was natural.

He pushed his trolley to the check-in counter and got his formalities completed before the madding crowd arrived.

He put his boarding pass safely in his pocket, and then headed to the book shop. He thought about buying something to read. The newspapers were full of bad news. Ash wrinkled his nose. Bad news and disasters attracted readers. Bad news sold papers. And papers wanted to be sold because they made money from advertising space and the advertisers wanted exposure. When he scanned the headlines, he felt a knot forming in his stomach, so he turned instead to the magazine rack. Then he reminded himself that they also made their money by selling advertising space. That wouldn't do. He scanned the book racks. No. Nothing caught his attention, so he decided to get himself a coffee instead.

He found a restaurant and took a seat at the window, sat down and waited to see what life had in store for him.

A young lady walked past him in a huff, headed for a table to his right. She looked troubled. She dumped her bags on the floor, sat down, dropped her head into her hands, and began to weep.

The waitress approached her, and through her tears she managed to place an order for coffee. Then she scratched around in her purse for some coins.

One fell on the floor and rolled away across the floor. Making a wide arc, it skirted between Ash's table and the wall and then, behaving like a meteorite caught in a planet's gravitational field, the coin headed back across the marble floor. But it didn't circle back to its owner. Instead, it turned in ever-smaller circles until like a whirling Dervish, it spun on its axis. Then it slowed and gracefully fell over.

"Well I never," thought Ash. "Who would have thought a coin could perform such a beautiful dance?"

Since he had conquered his fear of flying, Ash now loved planes. He found them graceful. But he still didn't like queues, so he waited until he was the last person to board. The cabin steward welcomed him and directed him to his seat. He patiently waited while the other passengers stowed their bags in the overhead compartments and then proceeded to his seat.

When he got there he found that it was occupied by the young lady who had been sobbing in the restaurant.

"I think you've got the wrong seat, ma'am," Ash said gently.

She protested loudly.

The air steward arrived and diplomatically resolved the problem. The young lady was indeed in the wrong seat. Hers was right next to Ash.

Once they were airborne Destiny got to work. She prodded Ash into action.

"I couldn't help but notice your sadness," said Ash quietly to the young woman alongside him.

"I'm sorry," she replied dismissively. "I guess I tend to wear my heart on my sleeve."

This was an evasion, and Ash knew it.

"Can I help?"

"Thanks, but it's a bit too late."

"I'm sorry to hear you say that," said Ash. "Fact is, it's never too late."

To be continued in

A Modern Parable Part 2

Ulysses The Fool.

Other books by P.D. Wells

Above Eden

Ulysses the Fool

The Incredible Meme

The Perfect Marriage

Authors note:

Dear reader.

Thank you so much for reading my book. I hope you enjoyed the journey enough to continue it with me. Ash is going to learn the most incredible things – and will become very powerful.

As with all information and advice, I encourage you to believe nothing anybody tells you. Check the facts, and then check again.

If you enjoyed reading my book please take a moment to leave me a review at your favorite retailer.

Many thanks.
PDW

www.ingramcontent.com/pod-product-compliance
Lightning Source LLC
Chambersburg PA
CBHW030936180526
45163CB00002B/594